Praise for
Leaving the American Sector

"Exciting, as you journey with Jeff on the daring and dangerous missions into Eastern Europe and Russia to bring the word
of God and other helpful materials to the believers inside the
Iron Curtain. Inspiring, to see what God can do through the
obedience and courage of one young man, willing to be led by
the Spirit of God. Proof that The Acts of the Apostles is an unfin-
ished book."

Chuck Smith, Pastor
Calvary Chapel Costa Mesa

"This is a page turner! I have known Jeff Thompson as a friend
and founder of EEO for many years. His heart for the widow
and orphan, and his determination to reach others with the
Gospel of salvation has been clearly evident in a life vigorously
lived for Christ. From the depths of despair of the abandoned
orphan to the heights of KGB and Kremlin power, this book will
inspire and inform you. It may change your life. This book
has a very important message for the American church."

Richard J. Broggi, Board of Directors
Pinnacle Forum America

"I highly recommend Jeff Thompson's book, *Leaving The American
Sector*. It is an awe-inspiring story of how God calls and raises up
modern heroes of the faith to share God's Word with oppressed
people. Having partnered with Jeff and Eastern European
Outreach since 1997, there is much more Jeff could have written about camps, children sponsorship, and educational scholarships. As Christians continue to reach out to people in need
with Christ's love, the magnificence of the EEO story keeps
unfolding."

Jeff Nellermoe, Senior Pastor
Good Shepherd Lutheran Church, Sandy, Utah

"I felt myself traveling with Jeff back behind the Iron Curtain to these distant lands. This book is packed with adventure and excitement and 'compassion that fails not.' Jeff's God is an enormous God, faithful to the very end. You'll be challenged to "live on" and realize at the end of each day...God is faithful! Jeff and Paula Thompson have an exciting story that will capture your attention and your heart."

Brian Bell, Senior Pastor
Calvary Chapel Murrieta

"*Leaving The American Sector* is a true testimony to the glorious goodness and grace of God. Jeff, Paula and the ministry of EEO have inspired many other ministries and mission organizations over the last two decades. If you read this book from beginning to end, God may inspire you to serve Him in wonderful ways you never imagined possible."

George Bryson, Director
Calvary Chapel Church Planting Mission

LEAVING THE AMERICAN SECTOR

JEFF THOMPSON

Theatron Books

Leaving the American Sector

Published by Theatron Books
An imprint of Theatron Media Group, Inc.
Post Office Box 606
Hemet, CA 92546-0606
Visit us at: www.TheatronBooks.com

All scripture quotations, unless otherwise indicated, are taken from the HOLY BIBLE, NEW INTERNATIONAL VERSION®. NIV®. Copyright ©1973, 1978, 1984 by International Bible Society. Used by permission of Zondervan. All rights reserved.

Cataloging In Publication Data
Thompson, Jeff
Leaving the American Sector /Jeff Thompson.— [1st ed.].
   p. cm.
  ISBN-13: 978-0-9747163-3-6
1. Thompson, Jeff 2. Christian Missions 3. Eastern Europe
4. Communism 5. Biography I. Title
BV3777
266' 0092 '4—dc22

ISBN-13: 978-0-9747163-3-6
ISBN-10: 0-9747163-3-2

Images: iStockphoto Agency

Printed in the United States of America

Visit www.LeavingTheAmericanSector.com for more exciting and inspirational stories about Jeff Thompson and the ministry of Eastern European Outreach.

Dedicated to Paula,
my partner in missions and in life
and to Lindsey, Joel and Grant
whom she raised so well
while I was away on
missionary trips.

Thank you, guys,
for loving me and making it possible
to leave the American Sector.

CONTENTS

Foreword, *ix*
Introduction, *xiii*

Chapter
1. Caught At The Border, *19*
2. Coming To Christ, *35*
3. A Bible Smuggler At 21, *43*
4. Missions Behind The Iron Curtain, *55*
5. A Dance Of Love, *65*
6. The Family Who Smuggles Together, *75*
7. The Battle Belongs To The Lord, *87*
8. Intrigue In Romania, *97*
9. After the Fall Of The Soviet Union, *115*
10. An Open Door To Russian Prisons, *123*
11. Spiritual Revolution Behind Barbed Wire, *135*
12. Children At Risk, *153*
13. The Balkans: Tragedy In Kosovo, *163*
14. A Changing Of The Guard, *177*
15. Full Circle, *189*
16. Into the Future, *199*

FOREWORD

Books, I read books, lots and lots of books and I enjoy them. I am so thankful for authors who take their time, effort and creativity to transport us to a different world, different cultures, and different experiences. Some do this better than others and usually I can tell in the first few pages what kind of experience I am going to have.

When I started reading Jeff Thompson's *Leaving the American Sector*, I immediately knew I was in for a very special experience. Although I had met him, I had no idea of the incredible journey on which the Lord had taken him. I was amazed how so many adventures and experiences have been packed into a relatively short life span.

I was hooked from the first page. I couldn't put it down and finished it in one sitting, something I rarely do. It is one of the most engrossing books I have read.

Leaving the American Sector fills us in on a very important aspect of the dangerous work that dedicated men and women did in a time when their stories could not be told. We forget the awful oppression, persecution and pain that those countries behind the Iron Curtain afflicted on their citizens. So many were living in darkness without any hope.

Jeff, in a beautiful, compelling and readable way, tells

the story of how he, his wife Paula, and others brought the living, inspired Word to so many. The Bible says that, "faith comes by hearing, and hearing by the Word of God." Those without that Word cannot hear, so cannot believe, cannot call upon the name of the Lord and thus cannot be saved.

Only God knows how many people came to faith because of these brave men and women, who risked their lives and faced long prison sentences because of their obedience and passion to see men and women hear the good news of salvation.

Leaving the American Sector is the story of intrigue, adventure, joy, sorrow, compassion, celebration and the faithfulness of the Heavenly Father to an ordinary couple, who believe in an extraordinary God.

The book encompasses various types of ministry, from taking Bibles and other Christian literature into countries where they were not allowed, to a ministry to those in prison, to providing education, to strengthening families. Jeff shares lessons from all these activities and demonstrates how, by keeping sensitive to the leading of the Holy Spirit, you can adjust to meeting the changing needs of people and society.

When he tells of the frightening stories of being confronted at various border crossings and facing years of imprisonment or perhaps death, his ability in sharing this puts you right there with him. I could see and hear the guards and felt that I was at his side.

I loved Jeff's story of his first fund-raising venture that, instead of raising support, put him in a negative cash position, as I had a similar experience. It was only one of the many obstacles that he and his family overcame, with the result that there will be thousands in heaven thanking them for sharing the love of our Lord Jesus Christ.

The book closes with the current social disintegration and discouraging conditions of many Eastern Europe countries and how Eastern European Outreach has a strategy to bring hope and love to those whom God loves in these countries.

It was my privilege to be with Jeff and Paula in Ukraine last year along with a number of others from Biola and all of us were so impressed with their ministry. Quietly, effectively and compassionately they were touching the lives of so many. To hear first-hand testimonies from those who have been introduced to the Lord Jesus Christ and are sharing His love was so encouraging. EEO and the other organizations working in Eastern Europe deserve and need our prayers and support.

As you start this adventure, I know you will be blessed and you will be drawn closer to the One, who is not willing that any should perish, but for all to have eternal life and to experience a wonderful relationship to the God who created them and sent His Son to redeem them.

Clyde Cook
President, Biola University
La Mirada, California

INTRODUCTION

I sit at my desk in Murrieta, California, as I write. Through the window I watch wheat stalks gently waving in a distant field. It's a timeless scene, a perfect picture seen virtually anywhere in the world this time of year. It's peaceful. The wind caressing the wheat can lull a person into falsely believing that wheat always bends gently in the wind and that times are always quiet. This isn't true.

It is my view that prosperity and the middle-class lifestyle anesthetizes American Christians to the needs of the world. Back in Soviet times, Christians suffering for their faith behind the Iron Curtain prayed for us in the West, that we would be able to withstand the spiritual burden of abundance. Affluence makes us feel good about ourselves, causing us oftentimes to miss the heart of God and His purpose for our lives.

For twelve years, from 1978 through 1990, I traveled and ministered behind the Iron Curtain. My mission was to strengthen the faith of believers there, the "persecuted church." As I reflect on that era, I understand that was the crucible in which my personal faith was formed. And in the midst of that missionary endeavor, a cataclysmic spiritual and political shift took place in Eastern Europe.

Winds of change began to blow there in the late 1980s. On November 9, 1989, the Berlin Wall fell. Oppressive communist regimes based on the bankrupt social theories of Marx and Lenin were toppled. The people were emboldened by the concepts of *Perestroika* and *Glasnost* ("openness" and "economic and social reform") that were introduced by then Soviet leader Mikhail Gorbachev. Gambling that the Soviets would not intervene militarily, the people of Eastern Europe rejected communism and embraced democracy. The Eastern Bloc nations of Albania, Poland, Hungary, Czechoslovakia, East Germany, Yugoslavia, Bulgaria and Romania fell like dominoes to the democratic will of the people. This shift in political power, and the speed at which it took place, was a modern miracle.

People were enslaved for up to 70 years by a ruthless and repressive form of government. Over 100 million people died at the hands of totalitarian dictators. Even in the darkest hours, however, faithful Christians behind the Iron Curtain worshiped and shared their faith, despite the imminent threat of imprisonment or death.

Tens of thousands of Christians outside the Iron Curtain prayed for these courageous believers and helped them keep the gospel lamp glowing in the darkness. These Westerners also sent Bibles and other resources through messengers who risked their lives so that these believers would know they had not been abandoned. I was one of those messengers.

The fall of communism brought freedom and joy to millions of people. At the same time, the Balkan region of Europe experienced war and poverty. The iron hand of dictators like Tito in Yugoslavia had served to repress historical ethnic hatreds in the Balkans. With new-found freedom, those hatreds reemerged and began to boil over.

Yugoslavia was formed after World War II, a patchwork of smaller countries that had historically held each other in contempt. Collectively they were known as the Balkans. Serbia, Croatia, Slovenia, Macedonia, Bosnia-Herzegovina and Kosovo were regions of distinct people groups and languages. As they decided to leave the Yugoslavian federation and return to the autonomy of their pre-World War II days, all hell boiled to the surface in a bloodbath of nationalism and ethnic cleansing

The same winds of social discontent that blew the Berlin Wall down in 1989 now fanned sparks of war in the Balkans. Serbia, led by dictator Slobodan Milosevic, was determined to establish dominance in the Balkans. After tens of thousands of people were killed, U.N. peacekeeping forces belatedly arrived in Bosnia-Herzegovina in 1995.

Sadly, the turmoil was not confined to Serbia, Croatia, and Bosnia. Further south two million ethnic Albanians lived in a little-known region called Kosovo. Even though the ethnic Albanians had lived there for hundreds of years, the Serbians sought to annihilate them and reclaim the region for themselves.

In 1998, an under-manned and ill-equipped Kosovo Liberation Army arose to declare their independence from Serbia. They were brutally crushed by Milosevic's Serbian forces. Thus began the ethnic cleansing campaign by Serbia which forced the Albanian majority out of Kosovo and into Albania and Macedonia. For 78 days in the spring of 1999, American bombers targeted and strafed Serbian military outposts, bringing the Serbian ethnic cleansing campaign to an end.

We do not often make the connection, but the Balkan wars of the 90s were another result of the fall of the Berlin Wall. Today, American troops and a U.N. peacekeeping force continue to preside over a fragile and artificial peace in Bosnia and Kosovo.

Winds of change are whirling again. Ukraine, the country that seems to have become my second home, tried to have a normal democratic presidential election. Though opposition candidate Viktor Yuschenko won the second run-off election held December 26, 2004, he was poisoned and almost killed in the process. Political freedom, as well as spiritual freedom, is still fragile in this part of the world.

In the midst of all this turmoil, Eastern European Outreach (EEO) has been there, sharing the truth that a better world can only come when individuals place Jesus Christ at the center of their lives. Through conflict and change, EEO has been distributing Bibles, caring for at-risk children, widows, orphans and prisoners.

There is still much to be done in spreading the gospel of Jesus Christ. I hope you will be inspired by this book to a deeper walk with God; and that you will partner with Eastern European Outreach to bring spiritual freedom to the people of Eastern Europe.

No book is complete without a sincere and heartfelt thank you expressed to all those who have played a part in the production of this book. For me personally, it has been a cathartic process, one lasting several years and riddled with occasional doubts that I would actually finish. If it were not for the help and encouragement of those around me, this story would continue to languish in the digital realm of my laptop hard drive.

Don Hughes of Theatron Books has been committed to this project from day one. He has navigated the waves of my indecision and doubts, and kept his compass on course to see this manuscript to completion. I owe him a great debt of gratitude for the editorial expertise he contriubted to this book.

Thanks also to our EEO staff in Murrieta, to Melody Monk, and to my mother, all of whose prodding and encouragement at various times reminded me afresh that this book needed to be written. I especially want to thank my wife, Paula, for supporting and encouraging me every step of the way.

To Oma and Bill, thank you for your hospitality and for the use of the cabin. It became my writing hideaway, one which I think every writer would love to have. To my lunch buddy Gordon, thank you for your prayers and encouragement along the way.

Thank you Lord Jesus for your guidance and the sense of conviction that writing this book was an act of obedience to you. It was written for your glory; I praise You for helping me to complete it.

Jeff Thompson
Founder/President
Eastern European Outreach

1
CAUGHT AT THE BORDER

It was a cold, rainy day in January, 1982. My assignment was to take a van loaded with Christian books and Bibles on an overnight trip from West Berlin into East Germany. I was traveling alone.

Our team had a yellow Toyota van that had been modified to run on gasoline or propane, and we had installed a large cylindrical tank in the back. It looked like any propane tank that commercial vehicles used in those days, but it was specially rigged to conceal Bibles and Christian books.

The tank looked normal from the outside, but you could take the heavy cap off the end and there was a large space to conceal things—big enough for a person, and definitely hundreds of books.

Inside the big tank was a small canister that was connected to a gauge on the outside of the tank. If curious border guards wanted to check the contents of the tank they could look at the pressure gauge, even open the valve a bit and smell the propane, though, unknown to them, it came from the small canister, not the larger tank. It was cleverly designed to look like the entire tank was filled with propane.

LEAVING THE AMERICAN SECTOR

That afternoon in Berlin, I loaded the tank with Bibles and Christian books requested by East German pastors, ratcheted the heavy end-cap of the tank onto the body of the tank, and prepared for my trip across the border. I had a little suitcase in the back with a blanket in it, items I would need later to deliver the books.

"Lord," I prayed, "I know you have called me to this ministry, and your people need your Word, so please calm my nerves and protect this load of Bibles going over the border tomorrow." After a night of restless sleep, Paula and I spent some quiet time praying together while our 6-month-old daughter slept. I threw my suitcase with one change of clothes inside into the back of the van, donned my jacket and gloves and left for the border.

I arrived to the border crossing Dreilinden about 1:00 p.m. The border area was well lit with extra searchlights placed all around the restricted border area. The misty monochrome afternoon was now punctuated by guard towers and machine gun-carrying soldiers keeping watch on the handful of vehicles desiring to enter the GDR (German Democratic Republic). They eyed travelers suspiciously, making them feel like criminals for entering their country. I waited, quietly praying, watching the vehicle in front of me being taken apart by suspicious guards searching for illegal contraband such as a German newspaper, a music cassette, or any type of printed matter.

A stone-faced guard in his drab, green uniform approached the van and examined my passport and visa. The tension was palpable, and the knowledge that I was crossing over into enemy territory, both figuratively and spiritually, was reinforced by a heaviness of spirit. Travel into East Germany and other communist bloc countries was not easy or joyful, it was tense and oppressive. Trying to look calm, my pulse rate quickened. There was no turning back and I had a tank full of almost 1000 books destined for believers in a prison called the GDR.

"Where are you going?" the border guard said in German.

"Magdeburg," I replied.

"What are you doing there?"

"I am just going to visit—I might like to go there on vacation in the future." Magdeburg was an industrial city in East Germany, not really a vacation destination, but such exchanges were a part of the ritual of border crossings.

The guard was asking more of the usual questions, when I saw that his attention was attracted by the tank in the back of the van. He became very curious about it, wondering why it was there. He began asking questions about it and had me open the rear door. He hit the tank with a crowbar and called over a couple of other guards to have a look at it.

One of them said such tanks were normal in vans converted to run on propane. "Just leave it," he said, much to the disdain of the original guard. I breathed a prayer of thanksgiving and hoped the search would end. But the original guard remained curious. He asked me to show him how the gauge worked, so I opened it and the pungent odor of propane seemed to bring his suspicions to an end.

I reached the outskirts of Magdeburg about 6 p.m. and checked into my hotel. The East German travel agency had to prearrange all travel details and they knew what time to expect you based on what time you departed from the border. There was no freedom of movement in East Germany and the Volks Polizei (People's Police) thoroughly patrolled the highways and exits.

I did not have much time. It had been dark for two hours and I was anxious to deliver my cargo. I strolled nonchalantly from the hotel and then walked briskly in order to discover if I was being followed. I doubled back to get the van and drove to a small country road parallel to the Elbe River. The place was symbolic to me. It was at this historic location that American troops under the command of General Eisenhower were ordered to wait while Russian troops arrived from the east to take Berlin and bring an end to World War II.

I had been trained to find a desolate spot to avoid being seen. I had to be sure I was not followed and that no one would notice me if they happened to drive by. I left the road and parked amidst the long reeds by the river, turning the engine and lights off. I got out and looked around, but did not hear any people or see any cigarettes glowing in the darkness. I heard only the quiet flow of the river. The night was pitch black and moonless. I knew I must work quickly.

I climbed into the side door of the van and closed it quietly behind me. It was dark and cold. Alone and vulnerable, I missed having someone to keep lookout for me while I unloaded the tank.

I removed the heavy end-cap of the tank, and began to unload the books onto the floor of the van. This was the riskiest step in the process, when the books were in the open. Although I might be able to throw a blanket over them, the end was off the tank and that could not be replaced quickly. I was in a desolate spot, but my mind raced and I began to wonder what I would say if a car, or God forbid, a police patrol came by.

With the tank now empty, I did my best to get the heavy cap back on the end of it, though it was difficult to do in the dark. I gave it a quick inspection by flashlight and everything appeared okay. I got out of the van, looked around one more time and checked my watch. 9:30 p.m. Time to get moving.

I drove to within 100 yards of the boxy, gray, nondescript apartment building. The suitcases weighed about 75 pounds apiece and I hoped the pastor lived on the ground floor. I found the apartment on the third floor and quietly knocked on the door. No response. I put my ear to the door. Nothing. I knocked again. No one answered. I was afraid to awaken or alert neighbors. I didn't want anyone to stick their head out of a door, hear my accented German, and immediately know an American had visited the pastor.

"Lord, what happens now?" I asked. I had the address of another pastor who lived a few miles away. It was now 10:30 and I had never met this other man.

"Lord, please may he be home," I prayed as I knocked on the door of the fifth-floor apartment.

"*Ja*," answered a tentative voice, cracking the door slightly.

I introduced myself in German using my fictitious name Bob, and our identity password, and asked if I could come in.

After allowing me inside, he led me to his small office. He was wearing his pajamas. His family was already in bed.

"Young man, how did you get my address?" he asked.

I explained that I worked for a mission group and that I had a load of Bibles and literature.

"Okay, let us pray together. Will you pray, please?" he asked.

While I formulated the words to pray in German, he was asking God if I was the real deal or not. He had to be cautious. Receiving and distributing literature could result in a prison sentence.

After prayer, he agreed to receive the books and asked where I was parked.

"Unfortunately, I must explain that most of the books are actually for another pastor in town. He was not home and yours was the only address I had."

"Don't worry. I promise that he will get the books."

I excused myself and returned with a load of books, huffing and puffing, unloading the suitcases while the pastor hid them behind a cabinet. He offered me a cup of tea, thinking that I was done. But I had to make three more such trips up and down the stairs before the van was empty. There was no time to waste. I worried that hotel security would notify the police that I had left and not returned. I also worried for this pastor. I was an unexpected visitor in the middle of the night with enough Bibles and books to put him in prison for several years. He was not accustomed to smuggling large amounts of literature.

"There are more Bibles here than I have seen in my lifetime," the pastor marveled. "I have never received so many books."

"Bob," he said, "here is an address. I will be staying there a few days next week in East Berlin. Can you come over to meet me?"

"Sure," I said, sticking the piece of paper in my pocket. "Let's pray for God's protection before I leave."

He prayed for my safe arrival back to Berlin and asked God to have us meet again. I prayed for his safety as well. As I turned for the door, we hugged, but we never met again.

I arrived back at the same border crossing I had passed through the previous day. A guard came out to begin the search. It was about noontime, and I was surprised to see the same suspicious guard from the day before. Normally he would have been off-duty, but his replacement was late.

The guard eyed me distrustfully. "I remember you from yesterday," he said.

"Yes," I replied.

"Where did you go again? Wasn't it Magdeburg?"

"Yes."

"How did you like it?" he said smiling. Magdeburg was an industrial city, not the sort of place that normally attracted tourists, so the thought that someone would check it out as a vacation destination had probably brought a question to his mind when he heard it the day before, and now the thought amused him.

"Oh, it was fine," I replied.

"Well, you came back so soon. You didn't have a good time?" After he said that he unleashed a torrent of intimidating questions.

As the questions came, my heart began beating faster. Every time you cross a border you always pray and ask God to blind the eyes of the guards and to confound their understanding. I had done that, but it seemed this guard was going to be relentless in his questioning and inspection. Perhaps he just didn't like the way his fellow guards had dismissed him when he questioned the purpose of the tank the previous day, and wanted to make a point with them. Perhaps he was tired from his long shift and just felt cantankerous.

Whatever the reason, he motioned to a nearby guard, pointed to the tank and said, "This tank is not original equipment. This tank is not supposed to be here. There is something wrong with this tank and I want to find out what it is."

The guard climbed in the back of the van and gave it a solid kick with his black boot. When he did, the end-cap of the tank unlatched. When he saw it move, he started yelling for more guards to come.

He climbed quickly out of the back of the van, grabbed me and pushed me up against the vehicle. "Okay, what's in that tank?" he demanded.

"I don't know what you are talking about," I replied.

The other guards came and began kicking the tank and the end cap began separating from the cylinder. It was obvious at this point that the tank was not really for propane, so the guard took my arm and pushed me into the back of the van. "Take that cap and pull it off," he screamed.

It was just hanging there, so I lifted it off and set it down on the floor of the van. At that point I wished I had secured it better the night before, but all had seemed well in the darkness.

The guards examined the interior of the tank with their flashlights. In the darkness of the previous night I had inadvertently left two books inside, and I nearly died when the guards retrieved them.

The persistent guard hauled me from the van and had

me stand spread-eagled against it and frisked me. Another guard came and together they escorted me into an interrogation room where I was strip-searched. They removed all of my clothes and searched every place possible for anything they could find, though at the time I was unaware that I had anything that would arouse suspicion.

After the body search, they kept me waiting for an hour, the posted guard eying me intently. There was no place to sit, so I stood near the heating radiator. I was trying to be nonchalant, but as time went by the gravity of my situation began to sink in. My knees began knocking uncontrollably. You hear stories about the level of fear that causes a person's knees to knock, or have seen it on TV, usually for comedic effect, but I never really understood the phenomenon. At that moment, however, my body began to shake and I had to grip my legs to keep my knees from knocking. I realized my emotions were out of control and I prayed that the Lord would calm me.

Finally, I was taken to another room. Two guards walked in and sat down. One guard motioned for me to sit down. He said in German, "Mr. Thompson, we have to fill out a protocol. You are a criminal in the East German Republic, and we need you to sign the paperwork."

I refused to sign the documents, fearing it would end my ministry behind the Iron Curtain. The guard who had offered me the pen and the documents gave me a sinister look when I rejected them. He said, "Sooner or later you will sign."

The guard began questioning me in German. I am fluent in German, but I felt like I needed to stall, to collect my thoughts, and to give the Lord an opportunity to intervene in the situation. Gaining some boldness, I spoke to him in German and said, "I am an American. My mother tongue is English. You must ask me your questions in English. I am not going to answer you in German. I am done speaking to you."

The guard pounded on the table and looked at me and

yelled, "I know you speak German. You will answer me in German." I remained silent.

He started to swear under his breath, but got on the phone and said, "Get me a translator in here right away." After a short wait an officer walked into the interrogation room. He was not an accomplished translator, but he knew some English.

The interrogator said, "Mr. Thompson, why have you come to the East German Republic?" Of course I understood exactly what he said, but I turned to the translator and waited for him to translate. The interrogator yelled his questions, but the translator wasn't mad about anything and conveyed the message in rather mild tones. He looked at me, searching for the right words, and said, "Well... Urr, Mr. Thompson, he wants to know why you visited our East German Republic." In the time it took him to translate, I had time to think about how I was going to answer.

"Tell him that I think it is a beautiful country."

He turned to his comrade and said, "He thinks it is a beautiful country."

The interrogator got angry again. This went on for nearly four hours.

At one point, the interrogator put his face inches from mine and said dramatically, "Mr. Thompson, we know you are smuggling cocaine. You are going to get eight years in prison for cocaine smuggling. So there is no reason to hide your information any longer. You must tell us exactly who you visited. We are going to find out, so tell us where you were and who you had contact with last night."

At that point, I thought to myself, if they wanted to plant a little bag of cocaine in the tank, it wouldn't matter what I said. If they wanted to imprison me they would. But our team of Bible smugglers had a commitment to always protect the identity of the believers in communist lands. That's a responsibility we assumed as part of our ministry.

A second time, about an hour later, he threatened me with being a cocaine dealer. But again, I knew my life was in the Lord's hands and it didn't matter what he said.

Finally, the interrogator said, "Mr. Thompson, are you a Christian?"

"Yes," I replied.

"Do you read the Bible?"

"Yes."

"Do you lie?"

"No."

"What does the Bible say about lying?"

"The Bible says you are not supposed to lie."

"So, tell me, why are you lying to me?

"I don't know what you are talking about," I replied.

"You do know what I am talking about."

The fact was, during the interrogation I could never be sure what he was getting at. I didn't want to lie, but it didn't bother my conscience to be evasive. I didn't want to incriminate myself by offering information too freely, and I certainly could not allow myself to be put in the position of incriminating my Christian brothers and sisters in the East.

It turned out that what really interested them was an address on a scrap of paper that they had found among my belongings during the strip search. The pastor who received the books said he was going to be visiting East Berlin in a few weeks and would like me to contact him while he was there. I had forgotten about the scrap of paper with his address on it, and didn't make a connection when the interrogator asked about it.

The interrogator asked about many different things, but he kept coming back to that address and that note. At one point I heard him say under his breath in German to the translator, "I know he is lying about this address because I have had lunch there before." He was a member of the East German Secret Police (Stasi) and they would spy on the Christians who gathered there. When I heard him say that to the translator in German, it dawned on me that they had found the piece of paper in my sock, and suddenly things became clear.

"The note you found was the address of a hostel in East Berlin," I said.

"Well, why did you lie about it?" he asked

"I couldn't remember what it was."

"Why did you have it?"

"Because I planned on going there in the future."

"Why?"

"Because I'm a Christian. I don't know if you believe in Christianity or not, but I look for opportunities to meet with Christians wherever I go. I thought perhaps I could meet with Christians at that place."

The interrogator turned out to be right—after hours of answering questions I finally signed the protocol that said I had broken the East German law, that I had imported contraband, Bibles and Christian books, and that I would not do so again.

They finally finished with the interrogation. The gruff officer said, "Mr. Thompson, you've signed the protocol. You have promised not to do this again. You have admitted to your crime of bringing in propaganda, so we are going to give you your vehicle back. As long as you pay the fine and don't do this again, everything will be okay."

A guard led me out of the room. By this time it was dark and he took me to the nearby impound garage where my van had been thoroughly inspected while I was being questioned.

The guard opened the doors of the garage and said, "Just pull out and park and someone will bring your passport."

I pulled the van to a parking space within the impound yard and I sat there for another hour. It was cold and snowing, and I was shivering because of the weather and because of the experience I had just undergone. I looked into the dark sky and said, "Lord, thank you for helping me through that ordeal."

LEAVING THE AMERICAN SECTOR

I could see the bright klieg lights illuminating the guard towers, and could see the guards walking back and forth holding their machine guns close to their chests. Freedom was on the other side; I was just yards from it. I thought about how East Germans felt, those who were trapped permanently behind the wall, separated from family and friends by barbed wire, and by guards with machine guns. They lived with that every day, knowing that freedom was just across the fence. They could see the sky over freedom every single day, but were powerless to cross over and enjoy it.

I was looking across the fence, longing for that freedom myself when a guard walked out of the office building with my passport in his hand. As he approached my van, he motioned for me to roll my window down. "Now, Mr. Thompson, you are not going to do this again, are you?" he said.

"No, I won't," I replied.

"Okay, be sure to drive carefully," he said as he handed me my passport."

Before I could reach up and put my hand on the passport, another guard suddenly rushed from the building and shouted, "Halt! Halt!"

The guard pulled the passport back and said, "Oh, I am sorry, I'll be right back. Just a moment."

He started walking away and I rolled the window back up. I had been relaxing a little bit, thinking the ordeal was over, but it looked like there might be another twist in the plot.

There was a rumbling and the double doors of the impound garage opened. Someone inside flipped a switch and the building was flooded with light. A guard, casting a long shadow, walked out and motioned for me to drive back into the garage. I did, and the doors rumbled closed behind me.

Two guards then suddenly rushed my van and started yelling, "Get out of the car! Get out of the car!" They grabbed me by my coat and took me back to the interrogation room.

I sat down in the empty room, wondering what new evil might have befallen me.

Two plainclothes Stasi officers walked in. The tall one was clearly in charge. His sidekick was the translator, and it turned out he was an excellent one. They began questioning me in the classic, "good cop, bad cop" method I had seen on television. The bad cop started by turning on the tape recorder and saying, "Mr. Thompson, you are a liar, aren't you?"

At that point, I didn't know what to say, so I said nothing. I was exhausted after the previous seven hours of questioning, bewildered by the new barrage of questions from this fresh team of inquisitors, and angry at myself for being duped by the guards into believing I was free. Still the torrent of questions came. Who are your parents? Where does your father work? What does your mother do? What do they earn? How many brothers and sisters do you have? How long have you been in Berlin? What is your address? What is your wife's name? What are your kids' names? Why are you here and for how long? Who does this vehicle belong to? Where did you buy it? How long have you had it? Why are you driving it?

The two men alternated in their questioning. One was angry, the other was nice. The bad cop would yell a question, the good cop would say to him in German, "Don't talk like that. Don't act that way." The good cop then turned to me and said in English, "Listen, we are not really mad at you, but just tell us who you were visiting because you're not going to get out of here. Make it easier on yourself, and that way you'll get a lighter sentence." Then the other fellow would yell a question again. It went back and forth like that for hours.

Finally, the bad cop said, "How many times have you crossed the border into East Germany?"

Was this the issue all along? Just the way the bad cop stated the question made me stop and think. That question had been asked before, but it seemed the man was actually waiting for a reply from me this time instead of drowning me in a cascading waterfall of questions. I was exhausted from the hours of badgering, and I thought maybe we had finally reached a crossroads. I tried to remember who asked the question the last time, but I was emotionally and physically drained, and had lost all track of time. Finally I said, "I'm sure it is in your protocol from the previous session."

"Well, just tell me. How many times have you been to our country," he said.

"I don't know exactly."

"Well, just approximately."

"I don't know. Five times or so."

"Oh, you mean five times last week, don't you?" the bad cop screamed, an expression of vindictive triumph on his face. He pulled out a three-page list and shook it in my face. It documented every date I had visited this side of the border in the last year and a half. The pages revealed I had been across the border over 60 times.

"Now tell me, Mr. Thompson, who do you work for?" the bad cop sneered. The insinuation was that I was a spy working for a foreign government. He was sure he had a big fish on the hook, and any hopes I had of making it across the border to freedom anytime soon were vanquished.

The interrogation lasted four additional hours, but it ended with a whimper rather than a bang. At about 10 p.m, I said, "You know, I have been here since noon and you haven't given me anything to eat or drink. I'm not going to talk to you anymore until you feed me."

The good cop said, "Oh, we are so sorry. We'll get right on that." A guard brought me a really terrible hot dog and a steaming cup of dense East German coffee. And that was the end of it. After I ate, they let me go. They felt like they had gotten everything they could, I suppose, and there was nothing to gain by holding me further.

As I pulled out of the impound yard I was apprehensive that this might be yet another trick, and that the guards would stop me and drag me back for more hours of interrogation. Two guards opened the gates of the chain link fence for me to exit, and as I passed through them I had a feeling of exhilaration, like the Children of Israel passing through the Red Sea to the freedom of the Promised Land.

Little did I know that this incident would start a cat-and-mouse game to trap and perhaps imprison me. I thought the game was over, but for the East German Secret Police, it was just beginning.

2
COMING TO CHRIST

Truman "Grandpa" Stogner grew up in the West Texas dust bowl in a poor, strict Southern Baptist family. His parents wanted him to be a preacher and insisted he go to a Texas Baptist college. This was an intolerable punishment in his mind, and early in the first school year he ran away and joined the Navy.

Six years later, now a seasoned sailor, Grandpa Stogner returned home to marry a young 16-year-old orphan girl named Dore, to whom he had been writing. They had their first child, Larry, on their first wedding anniversary. The Great Depression was in full swing when the little family moved to Texas to live with his parents. While there he learned there were jobs in the borax mines in the Mojave Desert outside Los Angeles, and he rode the rails to California and got a job there. He soon earned enough money to send bus tickets so his wife and child could join him, and later they settled in Long Beach, California.

My mother, Dian, was the youngest of their three children, and their only daughter. She was born and raised in Long Beach in a family dominated by Grandpa Stogner, who was hardheaded and proud. He worked industriously to provide for his family, but the Great Depression made opportunities scarce. He would glean the fields after the harvest, as was common in those days, to have food to put on the table.

Grandpa Stogner did well in marrying Dore. As an orphan she had learned how to "do without." She became an excellent seamstress, however, and always made sure her children were dressed respectably in a time when others were in rags due to financial hardship. The one topic that was not allowed in the Stogner home was that of religion. There was no place for God in their home.

My parents met on a blind date. My father, Jim, was a transplant from Chattanooga, Tennessee, where he lived on a small family farm. It was love at first sight for them.

After graduation, they married and soon began their family in the new suburb of Lakewood, California. My two older sisters, Andrea and Lisa, were five and three when I arrived on the scene in 1957. On the outside, we were the ideal suburban loving family. Inside the walls of our home, however, it was another story.

The tragedy inside the walls of our home was that my father battled alcohol and my mother ultimately vowed to divorce him if he didn't change. He didn't change, and the marriage ended when I was five. They loved each other, but they just couldn't make it work. After a few years, my mother remarried and we moved to Anaheim.

My mother considered herself an atheist, but that was based on her own upbringing more than intellectual conviction. Her parents had passed along their disinterest in religion to their children. As children, my sisters and I were not forbidden to go to church, nor did my mother speak unfavorably about God, but Christianity was ignored in our home.

As in her childhood home, religion was a topic seldom

discussed. At 15 years of age, I could only remember stepping inside a church once.

Nevertheless, God brings miracles into our lives. Emmy Lou Walsh lived nine houses down from ours, and she had recently become a Christian as a result of the illness of her brother, Mike. He was in the hospital with cancer, and they thought he was going to die. The family felt they needed a priest, but there wasn't one available. They called around, and finally found a pastor who was available, a young fellow fresh out of Bible college named Robert Pluimer, whom everyone called, "Pastor Butch." He was the minister of the tiny Colonial Bible Church in Anaheim.

Pastor Butch went to the hospital room and led Mike to the Lord. Family members called Pastor Butch and asked him to come back and explain the Bible to them. Butch began having Bible studies in Mike's hospital room and each evening the family came. Emmy Lou gave her life to the Lord there.

One day not long after, she walked down the street to visit and share a Christian book with my mother. What she didn't know, however, was that the previous evening my mother had watched a Billy Graham crusade on television. Mom wasn't sure she believed in God, but when the altar call came she closed her eyes and prayed the prayer of commitment with Billy Graham. My mother said, "I knew what I had done, I just didn't know what would happen next."

What happened was that her friend of seven years, Emmy Lou, came knocking on her door. Emmy Lou had a Christian book in her hand and asked if my mother was interested in reading it. It was then that my mother shared her salvation experience of the evening before.

Emmy Lou laughed, "That means you are a Christian now! Why don't you come to church with me?"

My mother felt Emmy Lou's visit was a confirmation that God had heard her prayer of salvation. Up to that point, Emmy Lou had never shared Jesus with her, and now, the very next morning after she had made her decision for

Christ, Emmy Lou showed up at her doorstep with a book to help her grow spiritually and an invitation to church.

Mom asked my step-father, Ken, and my sister, Lisa, who was still at home, and me if we wanted to go to church with her and Emmy Lou. My sister said yes, but my step-father said he had questions that needed answering first. I was kind of oblivious to the whole thing at that point.

So, the next Sunday my mother and sister attended Colonial Bible Church with Emmy Lou. I declined their invitation to go along. They both responded to the message that day, my sister for the first time, my mother for the second.

I remember coming home from school that week and seeing a Bible on our coffee table. I picked up the Bible from the coffee table and said, "What's this?"

"It's a Bible," my mother said.

"What's a Bible?"

"It's about Jesus."

"Oh," I said. I had grown up in Christian America, but at age 15 I had no clue what a Bible was or the nature of its contents. I lived in the midst of a religious void.

My mom said, "Why don't you read it?"

"Why would I read this?" I asked. We began to talk, but all my mother and sister knew was that you needed Jesus in your heart to go to heaven. Frankly, it didn't mean anything to me.

That next Sunday I decided to go along to church with my mother and sister. At the end of the message, the pastor gave an invitation and three young men raised their hands to receive Christ. One was Buddy Suitor, now a pastor in Corona, California. The other was Steve DeBerg, my sister's boyfriend at the time. He later enjoyed a 20-year career as an NFL quarterback. The third person was me. Driving home in the back seat of my sister's Ford Pinto, I knew something had happened inside but couldn't explain it. I learned later that I had been saved.

In the short span of a few weeks, our entire family came to know the Lord. Pastor Butch had visited my step-father, answered his questions, and he went to church and was saved. My elder sister, Andrea, was at college, but when she came home for a visit, she reported that she too had become a Christian. God's timing was wonderful.

Pastor Butch had an enormous influence on our family. As I got older, he took me under his wing and trained me for leadership. Rather than attending the youth or college group, I was included in the men's leadership classes. I was the youngest person in the group, but they never looked down on me because of my youth. They seemed to recognize the Lord was working in my life, and that His hand was upon me.

I was invited to another church. This one met in a tent and young people played rock music. My first Tuesday night Bible study under the canvas at Calvary Chapel in Costa Mesa was amazing. A sea of long-haired young people swayed and raised their hands as the musical group, Blessed Hope, played praise songs. Then Pastor Chuck Smith began the study in God's Word. For the first time I felt as if I belonged. The Saturday night concerts and the prayer times played an influential role in my early Christian life.

By 1977 I was 20 years old and had been praying for several years about becoming a missionary. I felt strongly the Lord was calling me, but I didn't know where. I began to talk with visiting missionaries and met with those who were going to the Philippines, Indonesia, and Africa. Although I was very interested, none of those places seemed right for me.

I was particularly discouraged when I spoke with missionaries to Africa. They asked me, "What do you have a degree in? What's your specialty? What do you have to offer the people, the society? They won't give you a visa in West Africa unless you're a doctor or have a particular skill that can be used to help the people."

I didn't have a degree of any kind. I had graduated from high school and gone to work for Capitol Pipe and Steel in Santa Ana. I didn't have any of the education or skills to meet the kind of requirements they had established. Yet I knew that God was calling me.

Paula and I are strong supporters of formal education—we have encouraged our children and others to get as much education as they can. Our daughter Lindsey earned her degree in speech pathology from Loma Linda University and is pursuing a master's degree. My son Joel earned his bachelor of arts in biblical studies at Biola University and is considering seminary training. When I was young, however, I sensed the Lord wanted me on the mission field. More than anything, I wanted to be obedient to the Lord.

I didn't know how to reconcile what others were saying with what I sensed to be God's leading, so I took my confusion to the Lord. I attended a retreat at the Calvary Chapel Twin Peaks Conference Center near Lake Arrowhead. I went to my knees in prayer and cried out to the Lord and He spoke to my heart. He confirmed that I was to go overseas, though I did not get clarity at that moment about the exact location. I got a very clear impression that I should look to the lands where there were persecuted believers.

The speaker at that retreat told a story about China as part of his message. When he mentioned China, he also mentioned Eastern Europe. My heart jumped. "Lord, is that where you are calling me?" I asked.

At that time, I had never read a missionary book or studied about Eastern Europe. I went to Pastor Butch and said, "I believe the Lord is calling me to be a missionary. What should I do?"

He asked, "Where is the Lord calling you?"

"I think somewhere like China or Eastern Europe, a place where there are persecuted Christians."

Pastor Butch looked at me intently, seeking discernment from the Lord. Finally he said, "I have a friend who has been to Eastern Europe. We'll go meet him, and maybe he can help you."

Pastor Butch took me to the office of Underground Evangelism in Pasadena, California, where we were warmly greeted by John Heck, who worked in the public relations department there. John and Pastor Butch had been Bible college classmates.

John turned to me and said, "Jeff, tell me what the Lord is doing in your life."

I shared how God had called me at Twin Peaks. John nodded and began to recount a story about Bible smugglers who were risking prison, perhaps even their lives, by taking copies of the Word of God behind the Iron Curtain.

It was at that moment that I had clarity from God about His purpose for my life, and tears welled up in my eyes.

John saw the tears and said, "Are you okay?"

Wiping my eyes, I said, "Yes... I just sensed the Holy Spirit speaking to my heart. The Lord is calling me to this type of ministry. This is what I am supposed to do." It was a life-changing moment for me. When I walked out of the office that day, I had the assurance in my heart that God had called me to serve Him in Eastern Europe.

A few months later I had the privilege of meeting Kees Van Olst, whom everyone called Brother Kees, and who was from the Netherlands. John Heck had arranged the meeting because he agreed that God was calling me to serve in Eastern Europe. John felt I might fit well into Kees' Bible smuggling operation, which was based just outside Vienna, Austria.

Our meeting was held in November, 1977, and I took the day off work to drive to Los Angeles and share my story with him.

When I finished, he looked at me and said, "Well, when

would you like to join our team?"

I was shocked. I hadn't thought that far ahead.

Brother Kees didn't want to stand in the way of God's call. He invited me to join their ministry team in Austria, and he figured God's call would prove itself. If I wasn't called of God I wouldn't last and they would send me home.

Brother Kees had a very positive attitude, in my view. Instead of questioning my age or education, he was interested in my spiritual gifts and dedication to serving the Lord. He didn't look at the earthly or human criteria for ministry, but instead looked upon my heart and sensed that God had indeed called me. He felt that the Lord brought us together, and I did too.

"When do you need me?" I asked.

"We needed you last week. Just tell me when you can be there."

This was the moment of truth. I had not expected to be asked that question. Praying about becoming a missionary is one thing, but to actually answer the call is another. I didn't need to pray about it any longer.

"I can make it in January," I said. "Will that be okay?"

"I will send you a letter of confirmation," he said.

We shook hands. I walked out to my car that day in a daze. I really was going to become a missionary! I had been accepted into the ranks of Bible smugglers at 20 years of age.

3

A BIBLE SMUGGLER AT 21

The Christmas of 1977 was especially emotional for me. The gift exchange included things I would need for my upcoming departure. Thermal underwear, gloves, a woolen cap, and luggage all served to remind me this could be the last Christmas with my family for quite some time. These items also warned me that, coming from Southern California, I wasn't prepared for the cold weather of Europe.

This would be my first trip overseas. Churches today regularly send people on overseas two-week mission trips, but it was much less common then. Now young people get a taste of what it might be like on the mission field, but I didn't have that luxury. The "career" word, however, was a question mark in my mind. I didn't know for how long God had called me to be a missionary. Was it going to be for one year? Maybe two? I would ask God this question every six months or so for the next seven years.

The letter of confirmation arrived just as Brother Kees had promised. Folded into a regular white envelope with a Vienna post office box return address was a plain letter typed in broken English.

LEAVING THE AMERICAN SECTOR

Dear Jeff,

Brother Kees made me known about your coming to our team. Send please details all about your arrival. We welcome you to our team and wait information from you soon.

The only return address provided was a post office box. There was no telephone number to use in case of emergency or travel interruption.

From November to January, this letter was the only information I had. Everything was shrouded in secrecy. I was filled with exhilaration and apprehension, and I was also filled with a little sadness. It was tough leaving. As I waved goodbye to my family, friends, and my girlfriend, Paula, whom I had known since the eighth grade, the reality of my decision hit me.

With only a post office box number on a envelope, I disappeared into the Lufthansa aircraft at LAX and flew to Frankfurt for the connection to Vienna. Little did I know that over the next 27 years I would make over 120 such transatlantic flights.

I arrived in Europe just a few weeks after my 21st birthday. I had no idea exactly what I would be doing. I only knew that I wanted to serve God and He had called me to Eastern Europe. I hoped someone would meet me at the airport, but the rest was in God's hands.

Two girls did meet me at the airport, Katie, an American, and Annika, who was from Holland. My flight had been delayed several hours and I was thankful to see them. I sat in the back seat of a small Peugeot as we careened along narrow, one-way cobblestone streets that headed outside the city.

"We aren't in Vienna anymore," said Annika.

I had assumed the mission base was in Vienna. That had been the postmark on the letter. The girls chatted in English, German and Dutch as we drove for 45 minutes to the large house where I would be staying.

Sabina, the cheerful team housemother, greeted me the next morning. "*Velkommen*, Jeff. How was your sleep?" She and her husband Ernst came from Switzerland and spoke Swiss-German, Italian, and a little English. They were in their mid-20s, and didn't have any children.

"Would you like corn flakes? I know Americans like them. We see it on television."

"Sure, thank you. I slept fine," I said, trying to be polite rather than completely truthful. The fact was I had slept terribly. Jet lag and my overactive nerves had kept me wired all night. As I ate my corn flakes, Sabina began to laugh.

"I am sorry," she said. "I don't mean to laugh at you. In Europe, we eat with both hands on the table. In America, you eat with your left hand on your leg. We always say that Americans have a gun under the table. You know, like in the old West."

I laughed and raised my hand to the table. "Where is everyone? Am I the only one here?" I suddenly realized it was already 10 a.m.

"Oh, they are working at the base, the warehouse. My husband gave you the day off today because you arrived so late last night."

After breakfast I went for a walk down the snowy lane to clear my head. My mind raced, trying to figure out where I was, what I was doing, and how to correct my table manners.

"Ahoy, Jeff," a tall man with hair as black as his leather jacket met me in the yard as I returned. He smiled broadly as he talked and shook my hand. His Swiss dialect was difficult to understand. It didn't sound like the German I had learned back in high school.

"This is my husband, Ernst." Sabina bubbled as she jumped down the steps to give him a hug.

LEAVING THE AMERICAN SECTOR

Ernst Meng was a tall, energetic young man. I quickly learned that he was our strategist, our "ops manager," the one who planned all the trips behind the Iron Curtain. He was very meticulous about his work; not only did he study the reports of those making previous trips, but he also delivered Bibles himself so he was familiar with the routes and contacts.

We all put a lot of trust in Ernst, and he was deserving of it. He chose the nationality of the various teams, the border crossings they would use, the routes they would travel, the vehicles they would use, the Bibles and books they would take, and the contacts to visit. He spent long hours poring over maps and praying.

I liked everyone I met. There were about twenty people on the team. The Swiss ran the office, the Dutch ran the garage housing the fleet of cars specially configured for smuggling, and the Germans ran the book warehouse. The Americans did whatever they were told.

I quickly discovered that many of the Europeans were somewhat distrusting of Americans. You had to earn their trust. These European missionaries were a mixture of students and families, all of whom had roles in the Bible smuggling ministry. There were a large number of vehicles involved in smuggling as well, including several motor homes, some camping trailers, and many vans and cars—each of them needing maintenance of some kind before being packed with Bibles.

My first assignment was to keep the vehicles prepared for missions behind the Iron Curtain. I was supposed to make sure they were mechanically sound, contained up-to-date registration and insurance papers, and that the oil was changed when needed. It didn't take long for them to realize that I wasn't a mechanic, so they assigned me to load the vehicles with Bibles. I worked with a young Dutch fellow named Willem. He had joined the team just three weeks before me and we hit it off immediately.

Packing the various vehicles was an important and

strenuous job. A mistake on our part could have serious consequences for the smuggling team. Every void was filled with literature, and I enjoyed loading the vehicles. We meticulously packed the books and Bibles in plastic so they would be dry and clean, then carefully concealed them in double floors, false panels, and other specially built secret compartments. I was working with a team to achieve the goal of spreading the Good News, and that was good.

One week after my arrival, Ernst informed me I would make my first trip with two seasoned team members, Ari and Dini. I looked forward to it. They were a robust and cheerful Dutch couple who ran the garage. They always spoke Dutch unless they were speaking to me and then we communicated with a mixture of English, German and hand signals. My German was improving, but very slowly.

Willem and I loaded the British-made motor home with a thousand Russian-language Bibles and books. It would be suspicious to have two single college-age boys driving a vehicle like this so Ari and Dini were the perfect couple for this trip. Ari was a 50-year-old missionary mechanic and his wife Dini kept our team well fed as the cook.

The next day, after a thorough pre-trip inspection, we gathered in the warehouse and joined hands to pray for a safe trip. "*Dank U val heer Yesus,*" they would pray in Dutch. "*Ameen!*" we would say in unison.

We headed for Hungary and a rendezvous with believers there ready to receive this shipment of Bibles. Ari drove the monstrous Bible smuggling machine while Dini consulted the map. I rode in the back of the motor home feeling pretty stressed about the job ahead. I did a lot of praying back there! Two hours later, we arrived at the border.

"Passports, please," said the Hungarian border guard. "You need visa, yes? Come inside."

After filling out the paperwork, we returned to the vehicle. The guard climbed inside, moved some cushions, looked inside our suitcases, opened the refrigerator, and asked for a cigarette. Within 30 minutes we were on our way.

"Thank you, Lord!" I shouted as we drove. We all laughed and praised God. In a few minutes though, the back-breaking work began. Once we passed the border checkpoint, it was my task to remove the books and Bibles from beneath the false floor.

The floor had eight carpet-covered panels that could be removed to reveal the metal floor underneath, including the area under the seats and table. As Ari drove, I crawled around on my hands and knees, pulled up the heavy floor panels and unloaded the Bibles. There was a lot of risk during the unpacking phase. Time was of the essence because Bibles were strewn everywhere and anything could happen. You didn't want to be stopped by the police for a speeding violation or a bad taillight. I threw blankets over them in case someone looked through a window, but little could be done if the police stopped us.

Every ten minutes Ari yelled, "Jeff, how are you?"

What he really meant was, "Jeff, hurry up! What is taking so long? When are you going to be done?"

Missionary work was harder than I had imagined when I was back home in California. An hour later, exhausted, I closed up the floor and secured the compartment. Our next step was to find a small hotel and wait for nightfall.

Beros Janos was a small, fearless Hungarian, a Christian man with a wife and three children, and he was dedicated to distributing Bibles and Christian literature to people behind the Iron Curtain. He was always happy to see us. He and Ari had an especially close relationship.

"Drive your vehicle into my barn tomorrow night and we will unload it," he said in German. "My neighbors know I have friends who live in the West. They will not betray me."

The next night we drove up in our very conspicuous motor home. Beros strode boldly out to meet us and we got right to work hiding Russian-language Bibles under the hay in his barn. I was impressed to be working alongside a true hero of the faith and was in awe of how God had such people working around the world. Here was the Body of Christ working to provide God's Word to others suffering for their faith. The moment is frozen in my memory as a perfect picture: a Dutchman, an American, and a Hungarian working together smuggling Bibles to Russia.

On that first trip I learned about spiritual oppression. When we crossed the border into Eastern Europe, I knew immediately that we were in enemy territory. It was a tangible feeling, a heaviness that didn't lift until you crossed back into freedom again. In the midst of that oppression, there were men like Beros, putting their lives on the line to provide light in a dark land.

My respect for men like Beros Janos and my youthful missionary zeal almost got me sent home after I had been in Vienna just a few months. In time I realized that Beros did not merely distribute Bibles in his native land, but was an integral part of a network that smuggled the Bibles further into the heart of Russia.

He used many ingenious methods to get the bulky books over the border en masse. One of them was befriending construction workers at a site that straddled the Hungarian-Russian border. They would load a dump truck with books, cover them with sand, and drive innocently to a safe location on the Russian side and unload them. Other members of the network would carry them in small bundles to believers throughout Russia.

No matter how ingenious or careful Beros had been, he came under suspicion and was arrested by the Secret Police. They did not have hard evidence about his activities, and they released him while they continued their investigation.

On one of my visits to him, he shared his great burden

with me. He was very aware that it was likely he would be convicted for smuggling, and that would mean years of separation from his wife and daughters; a thought, of course, that devastated him. He asked me to share his prayer request with people in American churches, with the hope that they might be moved to intervene politically on his behalf.

People in Eastern Europe had great admiration for Americans, and the religious freedom we enjoy, and they also had great expectations about their power to help them in particular ways.

In my zeal, I wrote a letter to Russ Chandler, religion editor of the *Los Angeles Times*, explaining the plight of Beros Janos. I suggested that Chandler contact John Heck at the Pasadena office of Underground Evangelism if he needed further information.

Little did I know that John Heck was shocked when he received a call from Russ Chandler. John felt that I had committed a very serious security breach by confirming that there was a Bible smuggling operation working out of Vienna. At the time, this would have caused diplomatic embarrassment, and could have resulted in the base being closed. John Heck wired Brother Kees in Vienna and told him to send me home.

Fortunately, even at that young age, I had the wisdom not to reveal important secrets. After all, that is why I suggested to Chandler that he contact the Underground Evangelism office for details. But one thing I suppose I did not understand at that point was the intricate balance between cooperating ministries and how easy it was to upset the apple cart. I was very much aware of the intrigue at the borders, but did not realize how deeply that intrigue was on both sides of the border, in governments and in missions agencies.

Brother Kees called me on the carpet. He waved the telex from John Heck in front of my face. He said they wanted me to return to the United States. He questioned me about my motives.

But, in the end, there wasn't much I could say. I loved Beros Janos for his commitment to Christ, and I wanted to help save him from prison if I could. I hadn't stopped to think of the ramifications for the entire Bible smuggling network.

Brother Kees looked at me sternly, then after a few moments shrugged his shoulders. "You will stay with us," he said. "But never do that again."

Ernst informed me I would be making a Bible trip to Berlin. He told me that our mission agency had a house there run by a young German couple, Burckhard and Renate. We would stay with them, reload our vehicles, and make a day trip into East Berlin.

The plan was that I would join him and Sabina, along with another Swiss couple. This trip required two vehicles: the motor home and the Plymouth. Lord willing, we would cross into East Germany to eventually join the other couple, Martin and Isabella.

As we made the ten-hour drive to Berlin, Ernst looked over at me, and, wanting to practice his English, asked, "Jeff, are you dirty?"

I didn't quite know how to respond. I quickly smelled my armpits. "Well, perhaps a little bit. Uh... yes, well, probably," I said, smiling.

Sabina, who had been lying quietly in the back, burst into laughter.

"What's so funny?" Ernst asked incredulously.

"Jeff," Sabina explained, "He meant 'are you tired,' not 'are you dirty!'"

"Well, I am pretty tired and a little dirty!" We all laughed.

LEAVING THE AMERICAN SECTOR

A few days later in Berlin, Martin and Isabella arrived. We then loaded the old Plymouth they were driving with more books and Bibles. Martin spoke no English, but Isabella did. They were both very friendly until the day of departure, then things became tense.

They were worried because I was new, but Ernst assured them everything would be okay. Martin was a nervous person by nature, but even more so when he was carrying Bibles. I discovered that many missionaries on the team reacted that way. Normally calm people became agitated right before a Bible run. I felt it was because of spiritual oppression that was so prevalent behind the Iron Curtain.

The border crossing went smoothly, at least in the sense that no attention was directed to the secret hiding place. Martin remained tense, however, but we all breathed easier after we received permission to proceed to our destination. After a long drive, we found our hotel, checked in, and later walked down the road to visit with some of the believers. We had the entire next day to unload the books and sort them for delivery to the different believers in our network. This was my first time in East Germany and the oppressive feeling I had sensed before was pervasive.

The next day Martin was feeling the pressure. He wanted to get the Bibles unloaded and delivered in a hurry. We picked what we thought was a desolate spot, but there were no trees for cover. I looked around at the rolling fields of corn. Surely this was a safe place to unpack the hidden books. Martin agreed. I unlocked the trunk and he climbed in to unpack the Bibles and I closed the lid over him. I went and sat in the car with Isabella. Once, a tiny East German-made Trabant drove slowly by and gawked at the American-made car from the 60s.

Martin fumbled in the near darkness of the trunk, a tiny flashlight clenched between his teeth. He struggled to remove the spare tire. He knocked on the trunk as a signal for me to unlock it. When I did, he quickly handed me the spare tire and jack. I closed the trunk lid again.

This procedure was fairly normal for us, but if there had been an onlooker around, all this trickery would have seemed pretty crazy. Perhaps it was!

Then Martin opened the hidden compartment. He was lying on his side in the trunk, with the lid closed, twisting and unloading books out of the compartment into the open space.

Isabella and I sat in the rocking car and quietly prayed. We kept an eye out on the road while Martin struggled with the books. We could hear as he grumbled about the whole situation.

Finally he had had enough. "Jeff, open the trunk! I need a breath of fresh air."

I got out, looked around, and, for the first time, noticed that a bus had pulled up behind us and parked just a few hundred feet away from us. The driver stepped out of his bus and was just standing there watching us.

I carefully unlocked the trunk with the key, opened it a few inches, and told Martin to be quiet. He was soaked in perspiration. He gratefully inhaled the fresh air, and dived back among the books. I closed the trunk and sat back down in the car while he kept working. The longer we sat there in the middle of nowhere, the more curious the bus driver became.

Finally, Martin was done. He knocked on the trunk for me to unlock it and release him from his airless dungeon.

"Martin, you have to wait. You cannot get out now," Isabella shouted with her hands cupped against the back seat.

"Why can't I? It's hot in here. Let me out!"

Martin became more agitated by the moment. We told him a bus driver was watching us and we couldn't simply open the trunk and have him climb out! I suddenly realized, however, that was only one of our problems. I patted my pockets frantically. Now I became the nervous one.

"Isabella, do you have the car key?" I asked.

She looked at me for a moment. "Jeff, are you joking? No, I don't have the key. You unlocked the trunk for Martin to get some fresh air, remember?"

"Yes, of course. I must have dropped it in the trunk in the middle of the books."

I had to tell Martin that I'd lost the key and that it must be with him inside the trunk. Martin was not a happy Christian, to say the least.

Isabella defended me when Martin exploded. "Honey, the bus driver was watching us. Jeff didn't mean to lose it!" She felt sorry for me, but I was worried about what to say if the police came along.

Suddenly people seemed to come out of nowhere to board the bus, and they stared as they walked by. Martin couldn't talk because a voice coming from a trunk is highly suspicious in any country.

I leaned nonchalantly against the car as people boarded the bus. It finally departed and I was able to turn my attention back to Martin's predicament.

In the meantime, God was merciful. Martin had found the keys among the books. I was able to lift the trunk a fraction of an inch, and Martin squeezed the key through the small gap. Arising from his tomb, he was soaked with perspiration and he strutted around like a wet hen before regaining his composure. He was mad and thankful at the same time. I was just thankful.

4

MISSIONS BEHIND THE IRON CURTAIN

I made many day trips into East Berlin during my early days of ministry with the Vienna team. After several trips through Checkpoint Charlie into East Berlin, I felt more confident traveling by myself. Berlin was a special place, a divided city where East met West. Tourists were allowed a one-day visa to the East side. The American army had a large presence in West Berlin, so Americans were commonly seen crossing Checkpoint Charlie. Unlike other East European countries, I didn't stand out in Berlin simply by being an American.

Despite my ability to blend better in Berlin, Ernst had other plans for me. He scheduled me for a train trip to Prague and a ten-day camping trip to Romania.

The trip to Romania meant pulling a camping trailer full of Bibles and it seemed problematic to me. It was only May, not yet summer vacation, so we might be suspect. My team-mate George was Swiss and he didn't speak English. He also didn't have a driver's license. I had a license, but I had never pulled a trailer before. Needless to say, I didn't like the plan and let Ernst know. It didn't matter. The weather had turned warmer and he wanted that trailer put into full use.

Before we left, Ernst briefed us with maps and provided the addresses of the believers. We had a very good smuggling network in Romania because the Christian churches were strong despite intense persecution. Romania's reputation of brutal border crossings, however, was well deserved. It was normal to wait hours in line for your car to be searched. The communists had no concept of customer service. They couldn't have cared less whether you entered their country or not.

"I am sending you over a very small border crossing that has just opened, and I'm not sure it will be an uneventful crossing," Ernst warned. "It should take less time, but you will be our first team there, so be sure to take good mental notes."

We left Ernst's office and drove to the warehouse. Ari, Willem, George and I examined every part of the trailer in detail, including the secret compartment.

Ari wiped the grease off his hands. "It's time to pray."

Amidst cases of Bibles, spare tires and motor oil, everyone in the garage stopped what they were doing. We all sought the Lord, each praying in his own language.

I had never been to Romania and I knew nothing of their ruthless dictator, Nicolai Ceausescu at that time. Before we departed on that fine afternoon in May, Dini corralled us into the kitchen for a final cup of strong hot coffee. "Be careful," she warned.

Ernst wasn't kidding. The Romanian crossing was tiny and we were the only vehicle there. After a 30-minute cigarette break, one of the guards sauntered over. "Show me your passports. Do you have any cigarettes?"

"Sorry," I shook my head.

"Where are you going? Give me your car papers."

"Bucharest," I answered and handed him the car registration papers.

He nodded and disappeared into the building.

Ten minutes later six guards returned accompanied by a female officer. "Mr. Thompson, you are from California?"

"Yes," I replied.

"I think this is your first time to our country, no?"

"Yes, it is."

"Why did you come here? And where did you get this car and trailer?"

Guards motioned for us to exit the vehicle. We stood facing the woman while they began to search the car. "We are just friends traveling together and we wanted to see Romania." I smiled while answering her questions, trying to remain relaxed.

One guard brought out a small toolbox, crawled in the front seat, and began removing the dashboard. Another guard opened the hood and asked for some tools. Still another was busy removing the back seat while a fourth rifled through our luggage. Two more inspected the trailer.

The female officer addressed George, "Come with me." She turned to me and said, "You stay."

I watched them go into the tiny office and I jumped when a guard shouted, "You! Come here and take the refrigerator out!"

I climbed inside the trailer.

"Empty your pockets," he said in German, motioning to my pants.

Addresses of believers, written in code on onionskin paper, were hidden inside my deodorant stick. Several thousand U.S. dollars, to be used to support persecuted Christians, were hidden inside a small fire extinguisher. I put a couple hundred Deutsch marks on the table.

"Take this refrigerator, take these beds out, and the table, everything that can be removed," the guard demanded. He then pulled up the wooden top to the storage area, which served as a bed. Right at that spot, underneath the gear, was the opening for the secret compartment. Under the edge of the linoleum were screws in the floor. Removing the screws removed the cover to the opening. He stared at the floor while my heart pounded. We stood there together looking at the floor. An eternity passed. "This is my bed," I joked. He laughed and put the piece of wood back in place.

When I pulled the refrigerator out, I noticed a guard lying on the ground underneath the trailer, inches away from where the Bibles were hidden. At that moment seven guards were actively searching us. "Lord," I prayed silently, "Your people suffering for their faith need your Word. Please blind the eyes of these guards to the Bibles."

The female officer came out again. George remained inside.

"Here are your passports," she said. "Please turn your car around and return to Hungary. Your entrance is denied."

"There must be a mistake," I said. "Why are you sending us back? We only want to visit your beautiful country."

"Turn around please—go back." She looked directly at me, turned and went inside.

I looked at my watch; we had been there for 2½ hours. I went inside to look for George and found him talking to a man in uniform. He winked at me to signal that everything was fine.

"Our entrance is denied," I told him quietly.

"Excuse me," the man said, "but can I help you?"

He listened to our story and accompanied us outside.

"We have been here almost three hours," I said. "We have done nothing wrong. We just want to visit your country."

"Let me see what I can do," he said. He returned to the building.

Ten minutes later he came to get us. "Bring your passports inside. You must exchange some money into our currency. You must change at least $20 U.S. per day, per person."

Within a few minutes we had exchanged money, restored the trailer and reloaded the car. During our three hours on the border, the guards had spent about 30 minutes searching very near to where the Bibles were hidden. On May 13th at 3 p.m. the bar was raised and we jubilantly entered Romania. We made the mental note for Ernst to never use that border crossing again! The Lord had answered our prayers, as well as the prayers of others around the world.

That night we slept on a country road next to a farmer's field. The next morning the battery was dead. The refrigerator had been plugged in all night, and we had used lights in the trailer. We flagged down a tractor, put the car into low gear, and the driver pulled us until it started. We thanked him with a bag of German coffee and some chocolate for his children.

Arad is a west Romanian industrial town. It is not a tourist destination and our trailer was conspicuous. Since we didn't have far to drive that day, maybe 20 minutes, we parked along the road under some trees. The cities in Romania had police checkpoints on main roads in and out of each city, and we didn't want to be seen. We spent the day reading, napping, and waiting for nightfall. We kept the refrigerator plugged in to keep the milk cool.

At 9 p.m. we began walking toward the outskirts of Arad. 45 minutes later we found the small farmhouse we were looking for and knocked on the door. Mom and Dad were not at home, but the kids had been instructed that when foreigners came, they should let them in. The children prayed with us and made tea. Mr. and Mrs. Popa came home about 10:30 with big "I-told-you-so" smiles on their faces.

"Do you come from Brother Kees?" they asked.

"Yes, we do," George said.

"We saw the foreign car on the road today and immediately started praying that a team from Brother Kees was bringing us God's Word. My wife told me that you would be here tonight, but I didn't believe her. Do you have Bibles for us?"

Everyone was excited. The kids sat quietly wide-eyed in the small kitchen. They smiled whenever we looked their way. It was a common story among the missionaries that Romanian believers would have dreams or visions of a team coming to visit. One team told of a family so convinced that they cooked extra food for dinner and set the table for two extra people. When the team arrived, the table was set and the soup was hot.

Mr. Popa paused to think and then said, "You cannot bring the Bibles here. My son and I will take you to your car parked on the road. You will follow us back the other direction away from town. About one mile down we will turn left onto a dirt road and make the exchange in the forest. Okay?"

Then Mr. Popa prayed fervently in Romanian. "Amen," we all agreed. In my mind, we were privileged to pray with another hero of the faith.

We crammed into his small Dacia, a Romanian copy of the Renault from France, and sped over a back road to bypass the police checkpoint to the main highway. He knew exactly where we were parked and we quickly jumped out into the black night.

I hurried around the driver's door, and made sure the trailer was hooked up and the lights plugged in. We had unpacked the Bibles earlier that day and they were covered with a blanket.

Something else had remained plugged in—the refrigerator! We had forgotten to unplug it that day and it had done a great job of keeping the food cool and draining the car battery.

We hopped in the car, nervous and in a hurry. Mr. Popa sped away, not waiting for us to start the car. I turned the key a half turn and there was no power, no dash lights, and no gauge movement.

I looked at George and said, "The battery is dead again."

"Try again," he said.

"George, look! The gas gauge is on empty and the battery gauge is below the red. Neither gauge is moving. We do have a dead battery!"

At that moment we felt the deep, unmistakable presence of the Holy Spirit in the car. I then turned the key all the way and the engine fired up.

I made a sharp U-turn, pulled the headlights on, and prayed that Mr. Popa was waiting for us somewhere up the road. But no, he had already pulled off into the woods. With adrenaline pumping, I turned onto the first dirt road I could find. The trailer bumped and shook over the rough road.

Finally, there was Mr. Popa on my right, surrounded by trees. I pulled up next to him and shut the lights off, but left the engine running, not wanting to take a chance on the battery. The Bibles were piled into the blankets and lifted into his trunk. Within minutes, the job was complete. We jumped into our vehicles and drove out of the woods in opposite directions with lights off.

As I think back on that night, surreal images come to my mind. It was as if the Holy Spirit had orchestrated a dance, and each of us was in our proper place for a moment in time, and then we were swirled away to other divine meetings.

George and I drove for two more hours that night. We watched the battery recharge itself and the gauges slowly move to their normal positions.

Our strategist Ernst and a co-worker, Alfred, decided to make a special trip to Russia through Berlin. Alfred was a slightly built German Bible college student with a reputation as a hard worker. The three of us met in Berlin at the mission base to discuss their trip. Their plan was to tape Bibles to their bodies using duct tape!

LEAVING THE AMERICAN SECTOR

The two men had shopped in Berlin for large overcoats, extra-large shirts, and baggy polyester pants. Then they duct-taped the Bibles around their stomachs and chests. They ended up taping about 90 copies each on themselves.

Small-print Russian Bibles were very compact in size. The Russians were prepared to cope with the situation, however, as they would use magnifying glasses to copy the Scriptures and pass them along. They were willing to do this because they valued the Word of God so much. Eleven years later, when the Iron Curtain disintegrated, the first requests out of Russia were for large-print Bibles.

Both Ernst and Alfred also carried four regular print Bibles. They taped some New Testaments and Gospels of John around their legs, and some Bibles on their thighs. When they sat down, they had Bibles below their kneecaps and above them, underneath, and on the backside on their calves. When they sat down in these polyester pants, it looked like they had square knees.

The only real problem, it seemed, was going to be the long drive. They had to cross the border from West Berlin to East Germany, and then from East Germany to Poland, and from Poland to Russia. The trip took 24 hours by the time they went through all the border crossings. You didn't simply drive over the border. You waited in long lines, were searched and questioned.

They had quite a story to tell when they returned. It seemed amusing at the time, but it illustrates the dedication of these two men, and how the Lord watched over them.

When they arrived at the Russian border of Brest, they were dead tired. The guards came out and asked them to remove their luggage from their car. They also asked them to remove the spare tire, the back seat, and anything else that could be removed. This was fairly typical. Doing it with Scriptures duct-taped all over their bodies was not.

They removed the mats from the floor and the guards began to look under the seats, behind the dashboard, and pulled off pieces of the upholstery.

It was when they searched the luggage that they found a Bible. Ernst had his personal German Bible with him in his suitcase. One guard took this Bible into the guardhouse. A few minutes later, an officer came out.

The officer asked Ernst, "Whose Bible is this?"

He said, "That's mine."

"Please, come in," said the officer.

After 24 hours of sitting with Bibles taped to his legs and body, desperate for a hot shower, Ernst followed stiffly.

He entered a little office with two chairs in it.

"Have a seat," said the officer.

Fighting the urge to say, "I would rather stand," Ernst carefully settled onto the chair.

The officer sat right across from him. He gazed at Ernst's face, then looked down directly at his square knees.

The official said, "Well now, we found a Bible in your suitcase. Is this your Bible?"

"Yes."

"Is this the only Bible you have?"

Ernst thought quickly. He determined that the Bible found in his luggage was the only one that he actually had a right to claim since the ones strapped to his body belonged to the desperate Christians in Russia. "Yes," he answered.

The officer continued, "We have been searching your vehicle for a long time now, a couple of hours. We've had other young people come to our country trying to bring Bibles with them. But we've been searching your vehicle and we can't find any. Are there any Bibles in your vehicle?"

Ernst answered truthfully, "No, there are not."

The official then asked, "Are you a Christian believer?"

"Yes," Ernst replied.

"Why are you a believer?"

Ernst told the official about his faith in God, and all the time he talked, the man looked at him, sometimes staring intently at his knees. From that angle, Ernst was sure anyone could clearly see the imprint of the Bibles on his square kneecaps.

They talked for a long time and finally the officer asked, "May I keep your Bible?"

"Yes, certainly, and I hope you read it," Ernst said.

They shook hands and the officer said, "Well, have a good time in our country."

Ernst walked stiffly but as fast as he could back to the car where Alfred waited. They drove off yelling and praising God, and later rejoiced even more when they could unstrap the Bibles and put them into the hands of Russian believers.

5
A DANCE OF LOVE

During those long, tense Bible smuggling trips, I always tried to keep my mind on the task at hand. It was not always possible, however. My thoughts often drifted to the girl I had left behind in America. Paula and I had met when we were both in the eighth grade at Crescent Junior High School in Anaheim.

She had long dark hair, hazel eyes, and a beautiful smile. What more could I ask? For me, it was love at first sight, but she didn't give me a second glance. We were 13 and I would fiddle with her hair in English class, trying to get her attention.

A big school dance was coming up and I had wanted to ask her to go with me. However, before I had the chance to ask her, she let it be known that she wouldn't accept. I was crushed and embarrassed. That was the beginning of my long wait for the shy and serious Paula Marie Banks to realize I was the guy for her.

That next summer I dreamed of Paula. I would watch her during our August football drills as she practiced across the field with the cheerleaders. When we began ninth grade, I was thrilled to discover we had two classes together: typing and German. A friendship began, and sometimes she talked to me. I think she enjoyed it, but I wasn't sure.

Most people attended the first dance of the new school year alone or with groups of friends. The school auditorium vibrated with the sounds of the Rolling Stones. Near the end of the dance, I spotted Paula across the crowded auditorium and walked over to talk to her. Her eyes met mine, she smiled and agreed to dance with me. She seemed genuinely happy that we danced the last dance together.

"What are you doing after the dance?" I asked. "Do you and your friends want to go to Shakey's?"

We joined several friends and walked together to the nearby Shakey's Pizza Parlor. Listening to Bob Dylan on the jukebox, hanging out, having Paula with me—I thought I was in heaven. While we waited for her parents outside, I slipped my arm around her shoulder. Her family's station wagon pulled up much too soon.

"Lynnette, who is that boy with his arm around Paula?" her father Leo asked with concern. This was the first time he had seen a boy with his arm around his 14-year-old daughter.

"It's probably that boy Jeff she has been talking about," her mother replied calmly.

Paula and I began to hang out that year. I played football, basketball and baseball on school teams. She was at every game cheering us on. We worked on our German homework together. I flirted with her in typing class. We went steady for our entire ninth-grade school year and she added stability to my life. However, unbeknownst to her, there were other influences fighting for my attention. One of them was drugs.

Drugs were prevalent on our Southern California junior high school campus and most of my friends were involved with them. I was not immune. I began to occasionally use marijuana, alcohol and various pills behind Paula's back.

After our ninth grade graduation, I spent every spare

moment of the summer of 1972 with Paula. With her as a girlfriend, I wasn't tempted to party with my friends. As my friends increased their experience with drugs and alcohol, I spent time at her house. As I look back, I can see how the Lord used her in my life even back then. That was the summer when I became a Christian.

Paula grew up in a Lutheran family. She had learned about the Bible, church and Christian things. I didn't have a clue about these things. We had never talked about spiritual things before, but when I got saved, I had many questions which I thought she could answer.

Paula thought it was great that I had become a Christian, but at the time her family was not regularly attending church. She thought of herself as a Christian, but had never really learned about being born again. I remember, though, that she certainly had more information about the Bible than I did.

Our first year in high school was the tenth grade, and our romance continued until the end of that year. She pursued cheerleading on the Savannah High School Song and Cheer Squad. I was pursuing the things of the Lord.

When we broke up, the Lord called me to a deeper commitment to Him.

I experienced the power of the Holy Spirit in a new way at a church retreat. The Lord was convicting me of my sin in a way I had never felt before. His presence and glory seemed to fill the room. A brother laid his hands on me and prayed. For over an hour I prayed and cried, oblivious to the others in our group. No message was given that night, but four people were saved from the 30 or so gathered there, and many more rededicated their lives to the Lord. I came home from that retreat a changed young man.

People saw the change in me. All of a sudden, I had the ability to say no to things that had previously tempted me.

My desire for God's Word was much greater and I also desired to witness, to learn, and to pray.

That summer of 1973, after the breakup with Paula, I experienced a major spiritual turning point. It seemed as if the Lord had brought her into my life for a season, and then removed her. I wondered if we would ever dance again.

"Hey Jeff, are you a Christian? Why don't you ever hang out with the Christians?" One of my friends, also named Jeff, was calling me to fellowship.

"I don't know, Where do they hang out?" I asked.

Jeff Augustine was the second Christian I had met on campus, and with his long hair, he seemed very cool. An ex-druggie, he had been radically saved and delivered from drugs at a church service there in Orange County. We began to study the Bible together after school. I became involved with, and later president of, the Christian club on campus. We trained fellow students to share their faith on campus. We showed films like *A Thief in the Night* and *A Distant Thunder* on Friday nights at the high school. About 75 students attended our lunchtime Christian club meetings. It was a time of tremendous spiritual growth for me.

Even though we were not seeing each other, Paula and I remained friends. She had another boyfriend, but just before our high school graduation, she sought me out one day on campus.

"Hi, Jeff! How are you? Hey, we have a new puppy at our house. What are you doing after school? Maybe I can come over and show him to you?

"Sure," I replied. The truth was, I was always happy to see Paula, but I knew she had a boyfriend.

The puppy was cute, but Paula was there for another reason.

"Jeff, I hope we'll stay in contact after graduation."

"Well, why don't you come to church with me sometime?" I asked.

Unknown to me, Paula was in the midst of breaking up with her current boyfriend and was interested in going out with me again. Soon she began attending church on her own and enjoying it.

During my senior year, I was constantly praying for God's will in my life for the future. I explored going to college and various career paths that I thought might be good. But at that point I had no real direction for the future. Most of my friends seemed to know what they were going to do after they graduated, but I was a bit uneasy about the future. I wanted to be obedient to the Lord about my future, but at that point I had no sure word from Him.

"Lord," I prayed, "If you don't open the door for me to go to college, then you must show me what I am to do. I am graduating soon and I really need to know."

I sensed in prayer that I was to simply trust the Lord for my future. During the last week of school, I found a job opening for a sales trainee posted on the bulletin board in the career guidance class. My heart jumped.

"Lord," I prayed, "Is this the job you have for me?"

At that moment Mr. Ritchie, the senior class guidance counselor, walked over and pulled the card off the bulletin board. "Jeff, how are you? I haven't seen you all year. I'm glad you came by. I have a job interview for you! This is a serious job, a career-type position. Would you like me to call and see if they are still hiring?"

A week after the interview, I felt the Lord showed me in prayer that I had gotten the job. I was so sure of this that I quit my part-time job at Longs Drugs that same night. I even told them that I was going to work for a steel company as a sales trainee. The next morning I was home when the phone rang.

"Hello."

"Hello Jeff, this is Ed Payne, western region sales manager with Capitol Pipe and Steel. We have made our decision and would like to hire you to work for us."

"That's great; thank you very much. When do I start?"

"How about starting Monday, 8 a.m.?"

"Great! You know, I knew you were going to call."

"You did? How did you know?" Ed asked.

"The Lord showed me yesterday that you were going to call. So I quit my other job last night."

A moment of silence followed before Ed replied, "Uh, well, Jeff, that's fine. We'll see you Monday then."

Within a week of graduation, I was working as a sales trainee with a large steel distribution company. Paula was training to be a legal secretary. We were each hired for $100 per week.

Capitol Pipe and Steel had never hired an 18-year-old for a sales position. Ed introduced me around and asked me to come into his office.

"Jeff, you are an experiment and we are going to give you a 90-day evaluation period. We have never hired someone so young before. We'll train you, but you also need to memorize the engineering standards for steel pipe and tubing. Here's the book. It's great to have you aboard."

My job at Capitol Pipe and Steel gave me valuable experience. After two years, I sensed God's call again and headed off to Europe to work behind the Iron Curtain. However, Paula was still on my heart.

We didn't have a firm commitment to each other while I was in Europe, though I did invite her to visit. Part of our mission team lived in a big three-story house outside Vienna, so there was plenty of space for her to stay.

While she was there Burckhard Rudat, the Berlin station chief, called Ernst in Vienna and told him he needed some people to deliver Bibles into East Berlin. Ernst suggested that Paula and I take a car and go help out there.

Paula was keeping in contact with her parents by phone, and she casually mentioned we were going into East Berlin. Her father, Leo, was understandably concerned. Paula handed the phone to me.

"Jeff, I am very serious," he said. "I want you to promise me that Paula will not go behind the Iron Curtain. Okay?"

"Yes Sir." I replied. "I understand. We are having a great time and I will make sure she doesn't go." I hung up the phone and looked at Paula. "You are not going to East Berlin. Your dad doesn't want you to. I promised him."

"Look Jeff, this is my decision and I want to go. I will talk with my dad when I get home."

She did go with me into East Berlin, used the German she had learned in school, and had the opportunity to see exactly the kind of ministry I was doing.

Before leaving America, I knew the Lord had given me assurance that Paula would one day be my wife, but He impressed upon me the need to be patient and not say anything to her. I thought the situation should just unfold.

However, a few months of loneliness in Austria after she returned home broke me, and I shared my love for her in a letter. This was a mistake, and, as I knew at the time, disobedient to the Lord's direction. Paula was still a long way from knowing if I was the one for her. I thought her visit to Austria might have clarified her thinking about me, but it hadn't. Her trip to Europe brought confusion, not confirmation.

I returned to the States in mid-December of 1978. My year away had been very stressful. I had been smuggling Bibles up to three weeks each month on trips throughout Eastern Europe. I also had admitted to myself that I was lonely. I hoped that on my visit home, Paula and I would decide that it was time for us to have a life together.

Within a few days of being home, I realized things were not as I imagined them. I had never asked Paula to make a commitment to me and I had not made a commitment to her. She had told me she would wait for my return, but during my absence she had met someone else. She wasn't technically dating him, but they saw each other often and she was very interested in him. Though she had visited Austria for a few weeks, I had been gone for a year. So it was understandable, but heartbreaking, to discover within 48 hours of arriving back home that she had a date with another guy for that first weekend I was home.

My third day home I received a call from my old company, Capitol.Pipe and Steel. They had heard I was back and wanted me to go to work for them at an increase in salary. My world changed quickly.

One short week earlier, I had smuggled Bibles with men whom I considered heroes of the faith. Then suddenly I had bounced back to my old life in Orange County. It was strange. I wondered what the Lord was doing in my life. I felt out of touch with friends. I wasn't comfortable in my own house. I was like a fish out of water.

A year passed quickly and by the following Christmas, Paula and I still had not decided to get married. We dated, but she also dated the other guy. Our relationship was awkward.

I wondered about God's plan. Maybe Paula and I were not meant for each other even though we had been friends for nearly 10 years. I decided it was best to just move on and see what God had in mind. If nothing was going to happen between us, maybe I needed to discover what else God had in store for me. It seemed logical that the Lord would have shown us by now if He intended for us to be a couple. I also sensed from the Lord that it was time for me to get back to Eastern Europe.

I prayed and knew it was time for "the talk." I shared my heart and told Paula I could see no reason for us to continue seeing each other.

"I am going back to Eastern Europe," I said. "I thought I would be going back with you, but it is clear this isn't happening. I cannot date you as just a friend, so it would be best if we didn't see each other anymore."

She began to cry. In her heart, she did love me, but her heart was divided and confused.

As the interim singles group pastor at my church, I had planned an outing to the Big Bear ski resort. About a week after "the talk" our group met for a 5 a.m. breakfast before going up the mountain. It was raining so hard they called off the ski trip, and everyone left the restaurant except for Paula and me.

"Jeff, can I talk to you?" she asked.

The last thing I wanted to do was spend time alone with Paula. It was too painful. That rainy morning, however, we decided to drive up the mountain, hoping the weather would clear for night skiing. The weather didn't clear, and we were able to talk about how God was working in our lives. Suddenly, after all those years, we discovered we really were of one mind and one heart.

"Jeff, I have been thinking, and crying, all week. I am not happy with the way things are right now." Paula's eyes cut through me as she spoke.

"I have always worried that you are called as a missionary, but if I am to be your wife, then I must be called as well. And I have never felt that calling like you do. As I thought about it, I realized that I want to be with you. Wherever you are is where I want to be. I don't know if you still want me, but if you do, I know what I want now. Maybe I didn't before, but I do now."

"Paula, I have always wanted you," I said. "But I have to serve the Lord. That is what I am going to do. If we are to be together, it means we will live somewhere in Europe, probably in Berlin."

"When you broke up with me," Paula said, "my thoughts began to settle. I couldn't eat or sleep. I have been miserable. I realized that I was called to be with you, and whatever that means, wherever we go, that's where I want to be."

We drove home from the ski lodge in awe of the turn of events. I asked Paula to marry me that night, and the next night we told her parents. Her father Leo was excited.

"Well it's about time! We were worried it might never happen!" Despite the fact I was taking their daughter away to the mission field, her parents were happy and supportive.

On September 13, 1980, I wept as I saw this radiant bride walk down the aisle to be at my side. I was the luckiest guy on Earth.

Nine years earlier, we had danced for the first time at our eighth grade September Sock Hop. Now, however, we got to dance again, and when I put my arms around her, her father proudly gave her away. We are still dancing.

6

THE FAMILY WHO SMUGGLES TOGETHER

Before Paula and I left California, I incorporated a non-profit ministry called A Bible for Russia (ABFR), which was the precursor of Eastern European Outreach. My desire was to do more than just raise our personal support. I wanted to flood Eastern Europe with Bibles and Christian literature. This was more than we could ask of our local church. So, with no experience and $2,000 from my savings account, we started this new mission agency.

Our church, Colonial Bible Church, provided the basis of our personal support. Pastor Butch asked for 60 men to stand up and pledge $10 per month to support us as missionaries. That was my only experience at fund raising! God blessed us through those men—we didn't have to do a thing.

We got on the plane and arrived in Germany with this new organization, ABFR, but we really didn't know how to run it. Our first mailing list was the people from our wedding list. I would type an occasional letter on our IBM Selectric typewriter, and mail it back to California. A friend, Dan Inversin, would make it into a newsletter and mail it to that wedding list. Some of these friends and family are still supporting us to this day.

Today the Berlin Wall is down, but in 1982 it sharply divided two countries, one which was democratic and free, the other which was under communist oppression. When I speak at churches today, younger people sometimes think that being a missionary in Berlin in those days was like being on a holiday. Many do not understand either the history or the spiritual oppression that existed under the communist regime.

After World War II, Stalin, Churchill, and Roosevelt met at the historic Levardia Palace in Yalta to divide up Europe into "spheres of influence." They agreed to divide Germany, and separately its capital, Berlin, into four parts or sectors. Each sector was governed by one of the victorious Allied forces: the United States, Great Britain, France, and Russia. Russia, however, our ally in World War II, began to enforce communism in the countries of Europe it dominated.

The city of Berlin was located inside the Russian-controlled sector, which became communist East Germany. A portion of Berlin was still free, however, controlled by the other three Allied powers. This produced a divided city. East Berlin was the Russian sector, and West Berlin consisted of the U.S., British, and French sectors. In terms of politics, Berlin was the world stage where two very different systems collided.

The Berlin Wall was one part of the armed border ringing the entire western half of the city.

Over time, this wall became a 12-foot-high, steel-reinforced, two-foot-wide, 102-mile-long barrier of death. The East German government built the Wall in August of 1961 to keep their people locked in a country much like prison. It became the symbol of the Iron Curtain.

During the 1950s, over two million refugees from the Russian sector flooded into West Berlin from the surrounding countryside of East Germany. Armed borders and the Wall put an end to citizens escaping to freedom. A fortress is built to protect from an outside attack. A prison is built to control or imprison those who are within its walls. On August 13, 1961, East Germany became a prison.

By the time we moved to West Berlin, it was a prosperous and rowdy island of freedom in the heart of communist East Germany, surrounded by Russian soldiers and East German border guards. This free island was a bustling half-of-a-city of two million people. What experts described as "the most fortified border in the world," surrounded this half-city. Those who lived in West Berlin endured a tense three-hour drive through the East German transit corridor, with two border crossings, before reaching a free West Germany.

To get to communist East Berlin and East Germany beyond, foreigners like us passed regularly through the famous U.S. Army-named border crossing known as "Checkpoint Charlie." The East Germans called it Friedrich Strasse.

I remember the first time I crossed. I looked up and read the warning, "You are leaving the American Sector." This prominent sign informed travelers in four languages that they were leaving a region of freedom and safety and on the other side hostile guards were watching every move people made.

Ninety feet within East Berlin, trip wires were in place to set off automatic machine guns. The standing order was "shoot to kill." The guards took their job seriously even though it was an order aimed at their own people, those unfortunate East Germans whose only crime was to desire freedom.

I focused my thoughts and prayers on those imprisoned by the Wall. Our organization had received a request from East German pastors. My job was to smuggle a load of

LEAVING THE AMERICAN SECTOR

Christian books, Bibles, and one-year devotionals to them on overnight trips from West Berlin into East Germany.

One month after our arrival in Berlin, it was time to apply for a residency permit. It was easy enough to obtain the permit; we just had to provide evidence of our employment. In our case, we were working under the auspices of a German mission organization, Osteuropa Mission, led by Burckhard and Renate Rudat, and a letter from them would suffice.

As the letter describing our employment was being typed, I loaded the car with Bibles and books. After our visa interview, we planned to make a day trip to East Berlin to visit Pastor Tschuschke and his wife, Doris.

At the immigration office we submitted our application, answered a few questions, and left. They never asked for the employment letter. We bounded down the stairs, jumped in the car, and headed around the corner for Checkpoint Charlie. Stopping to pray, we asked the Lord to blind the eyes of the border guards to the hidden Bibles, and thanked Him that the interview went so smoothly. We were excited, full of faith, and like a child who wanders in the street, not fully aware of the immediate danger.

Driving slowly by the sign warning that we were "Leaving the American Sector," I was reminded of how different everything was now. Paula and I were married. I didn't have to drive across these borders alone anymore. We were doing ministry together. She wanted to be there, by my side, bringing God's Word to believers. For someone not sure if she was called to be a missionary, she sure acted like one.

The barrier was raised and the soldier waved us into the border area.

He then disappeared into the small, gray, single-story building with bars over the windows. Guards walked around the car sliding long-handled mirrors on wheels underneath to search for contraband. One guard motioned to me to get out. They opened the car doors, the hood, the trunk, the glove compartment, and searched under the seats. Paula was still sitting in the passenger seat. A guard then reached in and began rifling through her purse.

As I stood next to the door and watched, I remembered the letter! It was too late. At that moment, he pulled an envelope out of her purse addressed to the Berlin Immigration Office. The guard opened the envelope and began to read the letter.

To Whom It May Concern:

"This letter is to confirm that Jeff and Paula Thompson, American citizens, have been invited to Berlin to work as Christian missionaries with the Ost-Europa Mission..."

The letter was on their nicest stationery and listed the telephone numbers, address, and bank account information for tax purposes, including their Federal Tax ID code. With this information, the East German secret police, the Stasi could learn everything about our activities. Though it didn't state we were smuggling Bibles, our mission base in Berlin had been compromised.

Unbelievably, the guard meticulously folded the letter up, inserted it back in the envelope, and put it back in Paula's purse. "I'll be right back. Wait here," he said. He entered the office building. I got back in the car. Panic began to set in and my heart was beating a mile a minute.

"Paula, we have to eat this letter."

"What?" she said. "Are you kidding?"

Tearing the letter in half, I said, "No, I'm not. It's the only way to get rid of it."

We each tore our half in half again, looked around at the

guards outside our car to make sure they weren't watching, and quickly stuffed the first piece in our mouths. It was nice heavy paper with a glossy finish, designed to impress the officials, but not intended to be lunch. Our mouths were dry. We were nervous. The more we chewed the bigger the paper became. It tasted terrible and didn't go down easily.

"Tear up the rest of the letter into small pieces; it will be easier to chew," I said with a full mouth.

We chewed and chewed. We watched the guard approach, accompanied by a woman guard. We swallowed just as they came to the door. I dropped a few remaining pieces into my coat pocket.

"*Komm mit!*" The guard ordered me to come along.

The woman guard took Paula into a separate building for her interrogation. Standing alone with the guard in a small room, he ordered me to empty my pockets. As the pieces dropped onto the table, the guard looked at them, then at me, and said "What's this?"

"Oh, it's paper," I said as nonchalantly as I could.

He began to try and fit the pieces together in order to be able to read the type, but was unable to do so.

"This is that letter I read, isn't it?"

Very quietly, I said, "Yes, it is."

"Why did you tear it up?"

"I didn't need it anymore," I replied.

"Where's the rest of it?"

"This is all there is," I said. Silence followed and I was worried. He carefully scooped up the remnants of the letter and placed them in a small plastic bag to keep as evidence.

"Mr. Thompson, what are you doing in Berlin?" he asked.

"We are staying with friends. We love Berlin."

My declaration didn't fit with what he'd just read in the letter, but he couldn't prove it. Besides, we had done nothing wrong. We had committed no crime. They realized that and released us both and we went back to our car. Eventually they raised the bar and waved us through.

We drove into East Berlin. I wondered if they had planted a listening device in the car. My thoughts raced about what we should do next. Should we go ahead and visit Pastor Tschuschke, or should we drive around the city and just go back over the border and go home? Were they going to follow us, or were they going to ask us questions when we returned to the border? Each option was risky. In the end, I decided to take a circuitous route to the pastor's house. We constantly checked to make sure we weren't being followed.

Martin and Doris Tschuschke had become close friends and partners in the ministry. We explained everything that had happened that day and told them we had taken every precaution to make sure we weren't being followed. However, we learned that Doris' family lived in West Germany and they often had foreign visitors. They weren't worried. They calmed our fears by their strong faith.

The border between East and West Germany had been erected while Pastor Martin was in seminary. Since Doris' family was on the West side, and they were students at the time, they had been given the option of moving back to the West. Martin reasoned there would be a great need for pastors on the communist side of the border, and they elected to stay and serve the Lord there. Now, here they were, trapped, yet encouraging us as we prepared to drive back to freedom.

Nothing terrible happened as a result of our unexpected lunch at Checkpoint Charlie. We don't believe we were followed. Pastor Martin did not receive threats or any visits by the Secret Police after our visit. The Lord supernaturally protected us.

Our lives had changed rather radically in a very short time. It was only 60 days after our wedding that Paula and I, surrounded by guards at Checkpoint Charlie, ate that letter. A month later, we discovered that Paula was pregnant. This was not part of our master plan, but it was part of God's plan.

Paula wanted and needed the security of being near family. I felt guilty about the situation. After all, we had just gotten married, left the country, and now I had to tell them their first grandchild would be born thousands of miles away.

During the turmoil of deciding where to have our baby, God used a letter from Paula's older brother, Andy, to take the burden off our shoulders. His letter was simple, and he lovingly said it would be great for us to come home, but would support our decision 100 percent, whatever it was.

After our daughter Lindsey was born in Berlin's Neukoellner Hospital, life took on a whole new meaning. I began to think about our future as missionaries, and how I would provide as a father for my wife and child.

Our son Joel followed just 15 months later. While we went through a lot of anguish deciding where Lindsey would be born, it was a much simpler decision the second time around. Paula was happy to have the care of the German doctors, and we were both glad when Joel joined us.

Our whole family was involved in the Bible smuggling ministry, including Joel while he was still in his mother's womb. We used to laugh about putting a Bible in Lindsey's diaper, but in reality, the Bibles were a little lower, in the seat cushion where the foam had been carved out. Both of us are forever thankful that our two eldest children were born in Germany where we were living and working as missionaries.

By the time our son Grant came along in 1993 we were no longer novice missionaries, but seasoned servants and we had a different view of things. We were living back in California by that time, and Paula quipped that she wanted to go back to Germany to have the baby.

We continued our ministry in Berlin, but back home

ABFR was just Jeff and Paula Thompson with some volunteer office help and support from friends and family.

A turning point came when I met Apollo 16 astronaut Charlie Duke at the "Berlin for Jesus" rally held at the Olympic stadium in West Berlin. I offered to take some of the main speakers at the rally to visit churches in East Berlin. Pat Robertson, the president of Christian Broadcasting Network, Loren Cunningham, the founder of Youth with a Mission, and Charlie Duke were among the group. Pastor Martin beamed that Sunday morning as these men brought powerful messages in his small church. Charlie also spoke at an unofficial youth gathering that afternoon.

Charlie proclaimed a triumphant gospel to the young people. He said, "I know the Soviet cosmonauts came back from space and said they didn't see God. But I am here to tell you today, that when I walked on the moon, looking at the Earth shining in the distance, I knew there was a Creator. I have walked on the moon, but I would rather walk with the Son. Jesus Christ is alive and well, He loves you, and invites you to give your life to Him!"

Charlie and his wife, Dottie, invited me to their home in New Braunfels, Texas, and to speak in their church. They arranged meetings and hosted me on different occasions, and today they still support the ministry. They were instrumental in those early days in helping to get the ABFR ministry off the ground.

Things changed in 1982 when the East Germans caught me and I feared my effectiveness was compromised. Paula began smuggling the Bibles through Checkpoint Charlie because I thought I might be followed. I also began to recruit U.S. Army soldiers to take Bibles for us into East Berlin. As part of the Allied Powers Agreement governing Berlin, they could cross over without being searched.

We began to attend a Bible study in the apartment of Chief Warrant Officer David Pizzimenti, a helicopter pilot. He and his wife, Kelly, were newcomers to Berlin and wanted to help our ministry. David had been a Chicago-area,

Mafia-connected drug-dealing transplant to Arkansas, and Kelly was a sweet young southern belle. They got saved, got married, joined the Army, and we met because I wanted to recruit them to smuggle Bibles. We became lifelong friends, and they went on to start a large, racially integrated church in southern Alabama before David went to be with the Lord in June 2004.

I had unfettered access to East Berlin, but after I was caught and warned, subtle changes began to occur. For example, almost anyone could go to the border crossing and enter East Berlin without too much hassle. Yes, they did inspect your car thoroughly and you could expect some delay, but the situation became different for me. When I would present my passport, the guards would make a phone call. I suspected they were reporting my movements to the Stasi because they would ask a lot of pointed questions, like the address where I was going, when I expected to arrive there and how long I would be staying. It was almost as if they were assigning a man to shadow me, though I never knew that for sure until years later.

I was able to work out several ways to overcome the threat of being shadowed, but over time the machinations became increasingly more ridiculous, and the danger and stress grew. For example, one ploy I used was to tell the border guards that I was going to visit an elderly grandmother, who happened to be a member of Pastor Martin's church. When the border guards asked for the address I would be visiting, I gave them her address. Grandmother Elfriede was thrilled that she could serve the Lord in this way. She knew she was helping the ministry and, at 80 years of age, could not care less what the Stasi might say or do. Certainly this was not an ideal situation, but it was one way of dealing with the increased surveillance.

Paula still had a clean record, of course, so she was able

to get through Checkpoint Charlie with relative ease, with Lindsey, just a few months old, strapped in the back seat. I would have to take the S-Bahn, the trolley system between East and West Berlin, because it was a way for me to avoid the extreme scrutiny of the border guards. We made elaborate plans for her to pick me up on the East Berlin side with the car loaded with hidden Bibles and together we would deliver them. She would have to drop me off before returning through Checkpoint Charlie with Lindsey.

As time went on, these plans became more elaborate as we tried to think of every contingency. If I didn't show up at the proper corner at the appointed time, she was to return immediately to the safety of West Berlin and wait to hear from me.

During this very stressful time, God began to reveal His will to me about our future. He spoke to me through a verse that was originally aimed at Israel. Romans 11:29 says, "The gifts and calling of God are irrevocable." It was as if God was saying to me, "Jeff, my gifting for you and my calling of you hasn't changed. My purpose for you hasn't changed. Whether in Germany or California, I have called you." God was preparing us for a change.

We loved the ministry and felt we were one in heart and soul with the persecuted people behind the Iron Curtain. I had not yet been blacklisted from entry into Soviet-controlled countries, but it was pretty clear that something was happening behind the scenes; though, at the time, I could not be exactly sure what it was.

It was clear that my usefulness was now limited, but I began to understand the real depth of the problem when I went to the Soviet Union in 1983. Paula and I were still based in Berlin, but I was making trips to Moscow. On one trip in I discovered I was being followed, and my room was searched as well. It was evident that I had been marked by Soviet authorities.

It was heart-wrenching to part with friends like Pastor Kurt Rogalski, Pastor Martin, Dave and Kelly and our many other ministry partners there. Nevertheless, in obedience we returned to California to see what God had for us.

7

THE BATTLE BELONGS TO THE LORD

Paula and I continued to learn that God was faithful. Having faith to cross communist borders with Bibles seemed easier than having faith for God to provide our physical and financial needs at home in America. Our lives had so much purpose in close fellowship with those suffering for their faith. In America, however, it seemed like people didn't have the time or interest.

"How was your time in Berlin?" someone would ask.

At first, we thought they really wanted to know. In reality, one-word answers like "good" or "fine" seemed to be enough for most people.

We changed the name of our organization to Eastern European Outreach (EEO). The name change was more reflective of our ministry to Eastern Europe, and not just Russia. I traveled to churches to tell people about the faithful believers behind the Iron Curtain whenever possible. When not speaking in churches, I worked part-time in different sales jobs to help earn a living. These were difficult years, but there were confirmations along the way.

"Jeff, would you still come even if we didn't take an offering for your ministry?" a pastor asked on the phone one day.

"Certainly. I'm not coming for money," I said.

"The Lord hasn't shown me yet whether we'll take an offering for you or not," he said.

"Pastor, thank you for your honesty," I replied, "I understand, and we're committed to being there." I explained that my Romanian friend, Radu, along with his father, would be with me. They were men who had suffered for their faith and who had escaped to America.

The pastor was touched during the service, however, and decided to take an offering after all.

He said, "As I was praying, folks, the Lord showed me tonight that your offering is not going to the ministry of Eastern European Outreach. This is going to Jeff Thompson personally, and Radu and his father. So whatever comes in we're going to divide it and give a third to each of them. We will also write a check out of our church budget to EEO to cover their travel costs."

They did that, and we each received $238. When I returned home to our little rented duplex in Corona, California, I discovered the refrigerator had broken and the car needed to be fixed. Those two bills together totaled $237. It was a small thing, but at the time, it was huge, because the Lord was saying, "Keep your eyes on Me; don't despair, don't doubt, I'm with you."

Some of the hardest lessons were not on the mission field, but at home. It was difficult to live like a missionary in Southern California. We were accustomed to the spiritual battle of crossing borders into the communist domain. We were not aware, however, of the spiritual battle we would face simply by living in America. This was a far different battle. The battle lines were not so clear.

We rented a small office on East 6th Street in Corona and the phone seldom rang. I would type the receipts for the friends who supported us on our only typewriter. We had two desks—one donated by family friends—a bookshelf and a telex machine. It is true that the results of our labor are in God's hands, but we also know that one "reaps what he sows." The principle of planting seed and expecting a harvest comes from God Himself. By 1985, after about two years of struggle to get EEO going, I was slowly losing heart.

I sent letters off to some of the larger churches in Southern California, introducing EEO and myself. The usual reply was either none at all, or a catalog of their teaching tapes and an order form. My time working at the steel company had taught me how to organize an office and work with people, but nothing could prepare me for working with churches. If they didn't know you, it was very difficult to get in the door.

As I boarded another flight, this time to St. Louis, I felt bad leaving Paula and the kids behind. Joel was two years old, Lindsey was four, and it seemed I was gone most of the time. We scraped by week-to-week and the financial struggle was wearing me down. "Lord," I prayed on the plane, "I don't think I have any faith anymore. I couldn't believe you for a pair of shoes, much less something really great."

The gentleman who picked me up at the airport informed me I would be staying in their home.

"So, Jeff, what's your fund-raising plan for the United States? Are you going to set up representatives around the country to raise money for you?" he asked while driving to his beautiful home in Chesterfield, an affluent suburb of St. Louis.

The thought had not occurred to me, nor was I comfortable talking in such a businesslike way about fund-raising. He led me to his daughter's bedroom, moved the teddy bear off the bed, and said he would be right back. A moment later, he handed me a brand-new pair of tennis shoes.

"Here, try these on. Size 10½. I think they will fit. They're yours. I am a sales rep for a shoe company and we had some extras. I bet you're tired. Take some time for yourself. Relax."

I thanked him, closed the door, knelt down beside the bed and cried. He had no idea what I had just prayed on the airplane. Again, the Lord was confirming His call and purpose for me. I had always thought that a person must have success if he or she is to be in God's Will. But I have learned God is not looking for success in our lives, He is looking for obedience. The results are His doing, not ours. With this in mind, I embarked upon another speaking trip, this time to Alabama.

Our friends from Berlin, David and Kelly Pizzimenti, had been transferred to Fort Rucker in the southeast corner of Alabama. Still in the service, David volunteered at a local church and invited me down there to speak. We also planned a fund-raising dinner banquet on Saturday night at the Holiday Inn in Dothan. David and his local church would get the word out about the meeting. I planned to show a film about the ministry.

We guaranteed 50 chicken dinners to the hotel and had free use of a meeting room. We decorated tables, set up the projector, set up the book table, and joined hands to pray. At 6 p.m. that night, only two people had arrived. David knew many more were on their way, so we waited another 25 minutes. Two more people showed up.

"Mr. Thompson, we have been ready to serve the dinners for some time now. What would you like us to do?" the waiter asked politely.

"Please give us a little more time," I said. "We would hate for these dinners to go to waste."

I looked at my watch. 6:30. Time for action. I moved to the podium and faced the two families that were seated at separate tables, surrounded by empty chairs in the large room.

"Folks, we have a much smaller crowd than expected tonight. It is 6:30 and time to get started. We have guaranteed this hotel payment for 50 chicken dinners. If Jesus were here with us, I believe He would go out into the highway and invite people in for a free dinner. Would you help us do that right now?"

We all headed for the street and began talking to people.

We invited them in for a free dinner and a movie. Ten more people off the street joined us that night. We ate, we laughed, I shared a short message, and some of them even stayed for the film. All during the evening, however, I was dying inside, sick to my stomach. The hotel graciously took ten percent off the bill, but we still paid close to $500 for the evening. We had raised $75.

I returned home after that speaking trip and added up the results. I had been gone for two weeks and the airfare, lodging and other expenses, minus the offerings, left us $129 in the red.

After two years of being home in the United States, I felt our efforts to support the ministry behind the Iron Curtain were going backwards.

"Excuse me, what do you mean they have denied my visa request? My flight leaves tomorrow! I will lose my ticket. Is there anything you can do?" I was upset, not because of losing the ticket, but because the Soviet Embassy had waited until the very last day to tell me I had been denied a visa.

"I am sorry, Mr. Thompson, I have been asked to tell you that your visa request is denied. No more, no less. Have a nice day." The consular official hung up the phone.

I was not fully aware of the reason for the denial of my visa at the time, even though I had my suspicions. It was not until after the Soviet Union fell that I was allowed in the country again.

I had arranged to travel with a small American team to Moscow and St. Petersburg to visit persecuted Christian families and collect information on Christian prisoners. The case of Christian rock singer Valeri Barinov was one we were investigating. We wanted to help. Now, the day before departure, I was informed that I had been denied a visa. I wanted to return to Russia and had prayed for the right timing but this evidently wasn't it. The team left without me, and it turned out that I would be denied a visa to Russia for another 6 years.

One of the families I wanted to visit were Russian believers whom I had met in 1981. I will never forget this Moscow family who lived on a 50-ruble-per-month pension (about $12 at the time). The father had given the best years of his life to the communist system, but having become believers, their income had been stopped by officials. Not once did this family request money or food. They had no refrigerator, and lived in a very small one-bedroom apartment. Their one request was for the Bible. Their daughter said, "Please, if you really care about us, bring us Bibles!"

There were days of blessing during this period, but many more days of discouragement. Brother Kees spoke to me on the phone from Holland. He said, "Jeff, you cannot quit. God has called you and given you a burden for His people behind the Iron Curtain." My friend was a fellow Bible smuggler from Europe, and was shocked that I was thinking of quitting.

"I know," I said, "but it just seems that we are not making any progress. Maybe the Lord has something else in mind for me."

"This is not a money issue. I think this is a faith issue. You must repent and place your trust in Him... again. He is faithful." He was right. I knew it deep down, but didn't want to admit it openly to myself.

"I can wait another month," I agreed. "There are meetings planned for next month. After that I'll make a decision."

Church meetings and a dinner banquet were planned in Illinois. I knew I should follow through on those meetings. Boarding the plane for the cornfields of central Illinois, I wondered whether this would be my last trip. The Lord seemed to be silent when I prayed.

John Lovell, a medical doctor, and his wife, Sheila, hosted me during my stay in Illinois. Sheila was a prayer warrior, and was certain the dinner banquet was going to be sold out.

"We are expecting 200 people," she said, waving her name list with phone numbers and verbal confirmations.

Her enthusiasm was contagious and soon she had me convinced of a great meeting coming up. Her faith and conviction were just what the spiritual doctor knew I needed. Sheila ferried me around, together with the youngest of their 3 boys, from meeting to meeting, which included Rotary Clubs, Christian schools, home Bible studies and appointments with local pastors. This Lutheran family loved the Lord and was amazed at the stories of God working behind the Iron Curtain.

Finally, Friday night arrived and it was time to head to Peoria and the smorgasbord restaurant. As we drove through the cornfields I couldn't help but be encouraged by Sheila's confidence. We were an hour early and began to set up for the evening. At ten minutes till six, the room was almost full. When I pronounced the opening prayer, there wasn't an empty seat to be found. As the meal was served, I squeezed in at a long table and introduced myself. "Hi, I'm Jeff Thompson with EEO."

"Hello, I'm Mrs. Jeff Thompson," the lady on my right said. We all laughed. Out of that crowd of 200 people, I had sat next to a lady who was also married to a Jeff Thompson. That night, the offering was in the thousands of dollars, more than covering our costs. Many hundreds of dollars were also pledged in monthly support of EEO. The tide was turning in the battle. Was I truly willing to live as a missionary in the United States? Was I willing to represent the cause and faith of believers behind the Iron Curtain? These were questions I felt the Lord was asking me.

"But Lord," I protested, "I cannot go to Russia anymore. How long am I supposed to be a missionary anyway? Five years? Ten years?"

I knew I had been called, but I always questioned how long I had been called for.

One afternoon while praying in my office, I heard this answer, "You are called until I tell you otherwise. I have been faithful to lead you thus far and I will not let you down. You don't need to ask me anymore."

"Yes sir. I understand. Thank you sir," That was the end of my questioning of God.

Around this time, a letter arrived from a law office in San Antonio. Unknown to me, EEO had been named as a beneficiary in the will of a person whom I had never met. They were requesting our corporate documents and tax ID number. I sent the information without giving it too much thought. Besides, nobody had ever mentioned anything to me about receiving part of his or her estate.

Eleven months later, I found the letter from the attorneys and gave them a call. "Yes, this is Jeff Thompson with Eastern European Outreach in Corona, California. We received a letter from you regarding the distribution of the estate of Mrs. Setrum. Do you have any information on this matter?" I asked.

"Yes, Mr. Thompson, thank you for calling. We just met with the executor of the estate yesterday and a distribution is going to be made next week among the four remaining recipients. That distribution should be about $80,000."

"Okay, great. Can you tell me what portion of that will be for EEO?" I asked.

"Oh, excuse me sir. That is your portion of the first distribution. When the estate is fully liquidated, you will receive a second distribution as well, though I do not know in what amount."

"Thank you very much," I stammered.

I had fallen backwards in my chair and had to get up off the floor. "Oh ye of little faith" were the words going through my mind. The total distribution amounted to $115,000 and was more than a year of support revenue for EEO. To my knowledge, I had never met Mrs. Setrum.

It turned out that Apollo 16 astronaut Charlie Duke, who lived near San Antonio and had arranged a few meetings for me there a couple of years earlier, had set the stage for this gift. The woman had attended one of those meetings, it seems, and the Lord had touched her heart.

8
INTRIGUE IN ROMANIA

Even though I could not get into Russia, I discovered I could get into Romania. Romania was an Eastern Bloc nation, but there were no Russian troops there. The country was under the iron fist of communist dictator and tyrant Nikolai Ceausescu, but Christianity was strong there. The rule of tyranny, enforced by the Romanian secret service, the Securitate, was strong as well. They spread terror and persecution throughout the country.

In the 1980s, in the the midst of this reign of terror, lived a 15-year-old young lady named Anita. Her father, Erwin, had been one of our Bible smuggling contacts for many years, and I had watched her grow up.

It was not easy being a Christian young person in Romania. Anita once told me how she had walked through the front door of her school and her classmates dumped a bucket of cow urine on her. As she told the story, her eyes were shining and she was smiling. Normally, you would think that a young girl would be embarrassed to mention such an incident—but she counted it all joy because she knew her classmates had done this to her simply because she was a Christian. This wonderful Christian girl had become the leader of an underground youth movement in the city of Brasov.

Erwin and I met in his small barn outside of town. He had hidden Bibles in a haystack there. I had delivered many loads of Bibles to this hiding place. It was the only place we could talk openly without fear of listening devices. Erwin had a brother in Germany, had learned the language and was able to speak fluent German with me.

"Jeff, bring your team to the youth meeting tomorrow night. The young people will be encouraged. Be careful that you are not followed, however."

I hesitated, but Erwin was adamant that we attend the meeting. "They will meet in a small A-frame cabin on the hillside above the city. It won't be easy to find, so go to the far side of the black cathedral in the town square at 6 p.m. Anita and her friends will meet you and lead you up to the house, about a half-an-hour walk from the square."

There were 35 people on our team, traveling by tour bus. It was difficult to be inconspicuous. Using buses was a rather new strategy we were testing. Bringing large groups on tour buses allowed us to smuggle in hundreds if not thousands of Bibles and lots of food and medicine. Romanian authorities were less suspicious of official tour groups than individual travelers.

The next night, the team left the hotel in pairs, at ten-minute intervals, and took different routes to reach the black church. Everyone arrived safely except me.

As I left the hotel, I walked through the square and noticed somebody was following me. I purposely paused at a shop window, and noticed the person also stopped. My heart began to race. I walked another 50 feet and paused again, this time turning and looking behind me. I was being followed, and this meant I could not meet the rest of the team at the church. If I was not at the church on time I'd miss the departure and would be unable to attend the meeting that night.

I walked a little further and stopped again. The man following me stopped also. I quickly walked around the corner and ducked inside a bakery. He didn't follow me, but waited at the corner. I bought some bread, and, mustering a little courage, left the bakery and walked towards him. As I got closer to him, he turned and walked in the opposite direction. He stopped at a shop window and I walked up to him and said in German, "Why are you following me?"

He looked at me and walked away.

I knew that I could not walk over to the church and expose the team to harassment by the authorities. Not being sure what to do next, I walked across the cobblestone square to another row of shops. At that point, I noticed somebody else following me, only this time he was not making any attempt to hide.

Dark gray suit, black shoes, slick hair, this guy seemed more professional than the first one. I guessed they were working as a team and had followed me from the hotel. I was now positive that I was not going to make it to the meeting. I began walking, and the new man followed me. After 45 minutes, I couldn't shake this guy. I would just have to return to the hotel.

It was quite a distance away, so I decided to catch a bus back to the center of town. I wasn't exactly sure where the bus was going, but I figured that it would travel to the middle of the city. I would simply get off somewhere near my hotel. There was a group of 10 or 15 people waiting to embark at the bus stop.

When the bus pulled up, a group of people jostled off and briskly disappeared. Those waiting elbowed their way onto the creaking, diesel-fume-filled bus shoving to find a place to stand. At the last minute, I decided not to get on the bus. Neither did the man who was following me. The bus left and there we were, the only ones left at the bus stop, standing 10 feet apart. The two of us just stood there and stared at each other. It was a chilling moment, one I didn't enjoy. However, as long as the team was safe and I wasn't put under arrest, then all could be well.

LEAVING THE AMERICAN SECTOR

Ten minutes later, another bus came by. It belched fumes and creaked to a stop. Standing-room-only again, and I had to shove my way in. I boarded through the back door and my Romanian secret police friend boarded in the front. I ducked behind people and waited. At the last minute, as the door was closing, I lunged out the door just as the bus was moving. Sweating, and alone at last, I stood there thanking the Lord for a few moments before heading towards the black cathedral.

Over an hour late, I didn't expect to find anyone there. I walked once around the cathedral to make sure, then started walking dejectedly back towards the hotel. I had gone just a few yards when Erwin walked around a corner, saw me, and called my name. I turned around and saw him wave at me. I rushed over and gave him a hug.

"Come!" he said. "We've been waiting for you. I came back one last time to see if I could find you. I prayed and the Lord said to walk around the church one more time, and that is when I saw you! Where have you been?"

I told him the story as we drove in his small jeep up the steep hill. The little house had been abandoned, and the youth group used it for secret meetings. It was well after dark and the meeting was underway with 60 or 70 young people in attendance.

The room was lit with candles and everyone sat on the floor and sang hymns in Romanian and English. It was a beautiful time of worship and prayer together, and we could sense the presence of God in our midst. Many people gave testimonies and prayer needs, and the unity we felt was incredible. As we quietly walked down the narrow mountain path that night, we all felt a sense of awe that only comes from being in the presence of God.

Romania was among the poorest of the Eastern European countries. So, along with Bibles, we always brought food, clothing, soap, medicines and anything else that families might need. Traveling by tour bus made crossing the border easier, and we could bring in larger quantities of supplies. Once inside the country, delivery of the supplies became more difficult. Official tour groups had Romanian tour guides assigned to each bus. Some guides were lazy and didn't care what the team did or where they went at night. Others were more like police than guides, asking lots of questions and investigating our activities.

Our team stopped in Cluj-Napoca for the night. Several deliveries were planned for that evening. After dark the team divided into groups of four, some delivering Bibles, others food, and others medicine.

Our guide ordered wine as he assumed the team would stay in the restaurant and party. At 15-minute intervals, different teams would nonchalantly yawn and leave the restaurant, talking about going for a walk before going to bed. I stayed and talked with the guide, keeping his attention away from the team.

A Romanian family in California had relatives in Cluj-Napoca, and had asked me to deliver some very expensive medicine to their mother who had been burned when a small gas heater exploded. There were no burn medications available in Romania and medical care was practically non-existent.

That afternoon I gave the address of the burn victim family to my friend Russ Bowyer from England, who had much experience in Romania.

"Russ, you have to get this medicine to this family tonight. It may mean life or death for the mother. She desperately needs it."

Russ did not know where the street was and neither did the taxi driver. They left the taxi and began walking through the dirt streets of the little suburb of Cluj-Napoca. They knew the approximate area from the handwritten map sent by the family with the medicine, but after hours of searching, the team was growing weary. The small wooden homes all looked alike, and many streets did not have signs.

Russ shared the complete story at breakfast the next morning. He said, "At that point, when we couldn't find the address, the team began getting frustrated. We had been walking around for a couple of hours. I even spoke to several people out for walks but nobody knew of the street. I didn't want to give up, but several team members were getting tired. Finally, we walked down this one small lane and ended up on the edge of town, in a farmer's cornfield. I looked at my watch and it was midnight."

Russ paused and sighed, reliving the emotion and desperation of needing to deliver that medicine and not being able to. "Well, we were at the end of the road and the end of our wits. There, at the end of that dirt road next to the cornfield, we gathered around in a circle to pray, holding hands. As we were praying, a passerby tapped one of the girls on the shoulder.

'I have information for you. Who are you looking for?' he asked in fluent English.

She let go of the hands she was holding and turned to talk to the gentleman.

'We are looking for this family, on this street,' she said.

The man pointed back the direction we had walked and said, 'That street is just over there. You are very close, just two streets away."

Russ's eyes got big and his face was full of wonder.

"The American girl said thank you and asked him to wait a moment, so he could take us there. She turned to finish the prayer with the group, and after we said 'Amen,' we opened our eyes to discover the person was gone!"

Russ said, "She was so excited, and said a man was walking by and told her how to find the street. She asked him to wait and help take us there, but when we opened our eyes, he was gone. 'I know how to find this street,' she said. 'Let's go.'

"Jeff, I really think this man was an angel. He spoke fluent English and knew exactly where to send us.

"The house was right where the angel had said it would be and the team was able to deliver the medicine. The wife cried and was filled with gratefulness. The family had no idea that medicine was on the way. For them the delivery of medicine was a miracle that saved the mother's life."

That morning at breakfast each team shared their experience from the night before. Russ' team, however, was the only one who had been visited by an English-speaking angel in a cornfield at midnight.

The Berlin Wall fell November 9, 1989, and, like dominoes, the governments of Eastern Europe followed. In Romania, the dictator Nikolai Ceausescu and his wife Elena were tried and executed on television. They each received one bullet to the head on December 25, 1989.

I flew in from California to Frankfurt on January 3, 1990. Burckhard, the German mission director from our days in Berlin, greeted me and we drove a vehicle stuffed with much-needed food and clothing. The next day as we approached the border near Oradea, we noticed that the guards were smiling. The flag hanging on the border was different as well. There was a hole cut out of the middle, where the hammer and sickle used to be.

The guard leaned in the window as he asked, "Do you have passports?"

We handed them over and waited.

"Go ahead," he said, shaking our hands. "You have aid for our people. No charge for visa. We have libertate (freedom) now!"

"Erwin, Erwin! Are you there? It's Bob and Andreas," we yelled as we reached the little house. Our Bible smuggling contact from Brasov, Erwin, cautiously stuck his head out the door. There were bullet holes just a few feet higher on his stucco wall. He grabbed us and pulled us into his small home. We didn't need to meet in the barn anymore.

"Erwin, are you okay? How is your family? Was anyone injured? You have freedom now," we said excitedly.

Erwin, however, was not so excited.

"Brothers, we still hear gunshots at night. We are afraid to go outside. We heard reports on the radio that the terrible Securitate is still fighting against citizens around the country."

"Erwin, you have freedom now. The borders are open. The Securitate are hiding and the police are looking for them. Ceausescu is gone. You can go outside and breathe again."

Erwin looked at us with disbelief, shaking his head. The terror in Romania had ended, but not the fear in people's hearts. We hugged and prayed, and gave presents to the kids. His wife fried some eggs for us. The haystack in the barn was never used to hide Bibles again.

In Timisoara, where the revolution had started, the secret police had dragged people through the streets. They electrocuted them, and cut off their limbs and heads as examples to scare and control the population. Over 2,000 lives were lost in Romania, as opposed to the Velvet Revolution in the Czech Republic where nobody died.

Later, in June, an EEO team from America arrived at the border with a tour bus with over forty people and supplies we intended to distribute to needy people. Peter, our official tour guide, was waiting at the border. He spoke perfect English and was a very nice young man. He was married and had a child. He had a job as an engineer, but moonlighted as a tour guide.

The team welcomed him and he became one of us. We would sing songs on the bus and I could see that he was very attracted to the unity and joy that he saw.

One afternoon, we stopped for lunch in the central Romanian town of Sibiu. The driver parked the large tour bus on the town square while we had our lunch. The bus attracted a lot of attention. A large crowd gathered to see what we were doing. There were about 100 people standing around wanting to talk with us. We didn't have our own translator and I asked Peter if he would mind translating for me.

He said, "Of course. What do you want to tell them?"

I smiled, "Well, I would like to talk to them about eternity, where they are going when they die."

"Oh, that sounds very interesting," he replied.

He did his best to translate a gospel message for the crowd, and he did indeed find it very interesting. After passing out Bibles and literature, we all got back on the bus. Everyone was excited and joyful at how the Lord had arranged this impromptu meeting.

Peter immediately got on the microphone and declared, "From now on you can call me Peter the Evangelist."

By the end of that journey, Peter gave his life to the Lord. For many years afterward I received postcards from him each Christmas. He lived in Bucharest with his family, attended a church and walked with the Lord.

In those days in Romania, as well as the entire Soviet bloc of countries, Christian belief cost something. A believer faced persecution, loss of a job, uncertainty for the future, going to prison, or being asked to deny his or her faith. That is what it meant to follow Jesus Christ. Not only was it an individual cost, but there was a cost to entire families. This actually strengthened the Church, and out of the suffering came great blessing.

A pastor and his wife, who miraculously escaped, once shared with me their perspective on the Christian life.

"We were not afraid of the authorities," they said. "We were afraid of not obeying God and His Word. We taught our small church that a Christian life that doesn't cost anything isn't worth anything!"

They truly caught the essence of our faith.

Taking our newborn daughter Lindsey for a stroll along the Berlin Wall. We lived daily in the shadow of these signs and the guard towers just on the other side.

Photo Gallery

After I was caught, Paula would place Lindsey in her backseat travel carrier on top of Bibles hidden inside the seat cushion. We prayed the guards would not disturb a sleeping baby.

Romanian shepherds posed for a picture with Paula during one of our Bible-smuggling trips. Paula was 5 months pregnant with our first child at the time and was excited about all God was doing in our lives.

Paula behind the wheel of a Citroen Ente, or "Duck," which could conceal 100 Bibles. We had to remove the rear wheel and open a secret compartment. We also used this car for smuggling secret documents about the persecution of Christians out of several East Bloc countries.

My good friend Burckhard Rudat was the West German mission director for Osteuropa Mission. Burckhard met me at an all-night café in Berlin and brought me home after I was caught.

Colonel Alexander Nikolayevich Dolgich, known informally as Sasha, was director of the 59 Youth Prisons in Russia. After our first trip, he took me to the airport and we joyfully sang together. He paused and said; "Jeff, when are you coming back? We have a lot of work to do!"

Colonel Dolgich on the left and General Sheriayev on the right grew up in the same hometown. Sheriayev invited me to go bear-hunting in the Urals and gave me a large hunting knife as a present.

It was common for prisoners to come forward and ask to have their Bibles autographed. We distributed literally hundreds of thousands of Bibles and Christian books with the help of a Christian businessman in Southern California, Jim Hodges of Royal Paper Box Company.

These Austrian soldiers , part of the U.N. peacekeeping force in Kosovo, posed for a quick picture with me before escorting us up a mountain to deliver aid to a remote village.

The Begaj family of Banje, Kosovo, on the gymnasium floor in Tirana, Albania, with 3,000 other refugees. Iliaz, the grandfather on the right, with Ramsia next to me and her sister Shevria and Ramsia's five children.

Brad Warren and I in front of the destroyed town of Gjakova, Kosovo, just days after the Serbian troops had retreated.

We traveled in this old Lada along muddy roads to minister to prisoners in a remote Siberian prison. The four Russian evangelists had faith that the car would make the treacherous trip, and it did.

The children of Chernobyl at one of our ministry centers. The drawing of a skeleton represents the death cloud of radiation covering the area as drawn by a child refugee evacuated from his home.

Lois Fonda of Rye, New Hampshire, an EEO New England representative, continues to touch lives around the world. Most team members have a hard time keeping up with her.

Irina Skypnyk and husband Yuri stand on either side of Paula. Irina has been our Ukraine director since 1994 and has been instrumental in navigating the Ukrainian bureaucracy and culture to bring about effective and efficient ministries to children.

L-to-R Grant, Joel, Lindsey, and Danielle, our late-in-life adopted daughter, all of us posing for a shot on a lifeguard tower at Newport Beach, California. As natives of Southern California, we of course love the beach.

9
AFTER THE FALL OF THE SOVIET UNION

By 1988-89, the policies of *Glasnost* and *Perestroika* were taking hold in the former Soviet Union, and society was slowly opening up. There was a lot of distrust among the people, however. Most were happy about the new freedom they were receiving, but it was alien to them and they were cautious about embracing it.

There was also a fear among some that there might be a sudden reversal and that all the reforms would be wiped away overnight by a military revolt. There was a great uneasiness among the people.

Though I was still denied an entry visa, EEO, through our missionary staff in Europe, distributed tens of thousands of Bibles in public evangelistic campaigns. This had not been possible for 70 years.

Back in California, I made contact with the High Flight Foundation in Colorado Springs. Another Christian astronaut, Apollo 15's Jim Irwin, had started this mission group a few years previously. During the time of the new openness in Russia, Jim had traveled there for speaking engagements.

He would ask groups, "Would you like your own Bible?" Virtually everyone in the crowd would raise their hand and he collected tens of thousands of Russian names and addresses.

Jim had not expected such a huge response, and they were faced with the challenge of fulfilling all the requests. EEO was already mailing Bibles to people in Russia, so I called and asked if they needed help.

He said, "Yes, absolutely!" EEO distributed many thousands of Bibles to the addresses the High Flight Foundation provided. Cooperation between the two ministries was wonderful.

One day the phone rang and Paula answered.

"Hello, this is Jim Irwin. I'm going to be speaking in Palm Springs, and I notice it's not too far from where you live. I'd love to come by and see your base of operations."

Paula chuckled to herself and said, "Did you know that our base of operations is in our home?"

He said, "That's okay. I'd really love to come by and meet you and your husband."

Paula invited him to lunch and he accepted. A few weeks later he arrived at our door in his NASA jumpsuit. We took eight-year-old Lindsey out of school to meet the Apollo astronaut. We had lunch and a wonderful time sharing the Lord together.

Due to a sudden heart attack, Jim went to be with the Lord just one year later. Jim's sincerity and humility is something we will never forget. He encouraged us in the Lord, and the Lord used this project to bring thousands of new ministry friends to EEO.

Anna Chertkova, a Russian believer, was arrested and taken into custody in 1972. Her crime was "circulation of false statements and slander against the Soviet state and social system." This was a common charge used against Christians and human rights activists during the Soviet era. Her real crime was that she had refused to compromise her faith. She maintained a bold Christian witness in her community. Anna's religious convictions rankled the atheistic authorities, and she was placed in an institution for the insane.

Ten years later in 1982, Anna's mother said, "Our daughter witnessed about her faith in God to others in public and this led to her confinement. She was arrested in 1972 and put in a psychiatric hospital. Ten years later, she is still there. She has complete control over her faculties, but is refused release because she maintains her belief in God."

If Anna had been sent to prison instead of a psychiatric hospital for her "anti-Soviet slander," she would have been released after only four years.

The extensive network of "psycho-prisons" included over 100 psychiatric hospitals for the criminally insane. Ringed by barbed wire and watchtowers, all medical personnel were officers of the Soviet secret police. Anna was just one of thousands of people who had vanished from Soviet society because of their faith.

Miraculously, a ray of hope emerged from the horrors of her drug-induced confinement when a letter, which had been smuggled from her tiny concrete cell, asked for intercessors to "call upon God for His will to be done in my life."

I contacted Bonnie Steffen, associate editor of the *Christian Reader* magazine in Wheaton, Illinois. I told her of Anna's fate, and asked if they would be willing to run a story asking their readers to send postcards to then Soviet leader Mikhail Gorbachev, asking for Anna's release. Bonnie was somewhat hesitant, but she agreed to consider the request and asked me to send her the story. The magazine did not normally run stories that called their subscribers to action, and inserted cards were usually for advertising purposes.

I sat at my desk in the tiny back bedroom of our home in Sun City, California, and began to write Anna's story, "Postmarked for Moscow." I asked readers to pray for Anna, and to send a postcard on her behalf. We also asked them to send a postcard to our EEO office, confirming they had sent the card to Moscow. Over three thousand cards flowed into our post office box, and within 90 days of publication of that article Anna was released from prison. We were one of several missions lobbying for her release, and I am thankful to God for the small part Eastern European Outreach had in helping Anna.

Several times when she had appeared before Soviet review panels she was told, "Deny God and you'll be home tomorrow." She never did deny God; nevertheless, He brought her home anyway.

God blessed EEO through our desire to help Anna. One of the most wonderful aspects of that blessing is that we had the opportunity to meet many new friends who were interested in helping the persecuted people of Eastern Europe.

One such person was Lois Fonda, who, at the time, was a 65-year-old widow from New Hampshire. She picked up a *Christian Reader* from the literature table in the foyer of her church, read the article, and was moved to action.

Later, she received an invitation from us to go on an outreach to the Soviet Union, and was one of the 46 people to sign up.

I recall that her church family, as well as her real family, thought she was crazy to traipse off to a dangerous country like the Soviet Union. But the fact is, as of this writing, Lois is in her 80s and has been to Eastern Europe about 48 times. In 2002 she had quadruple bypass heart surgery, but has been on at least six trips since then. Lois' enthusiasm and encouragement have always been blessings to me and others at EEO.

As the former Soviet Union began to open more, I began to arrange group mission trips. I still did not know whether I would actually be part of a group or not. However, in April

1990, I received a visa to the former Soviet Union for the first time since 1984.

We chartered a bus in Frankfurt, Germany, and our team began a long journey to take 3,000 Bibles to the former Soviet Union. We visited Dresden, Berlin, and Krakow; traveled on to Kiev and Odessa; went through Moldova, Romania and Hungary; and then returned to Frankfurt. Our worship on that bus was powerful and sweet.

On my next trip, just a few months later, I was detained at the border. I was by myself this time, flying from Helsinki to Riga, Latvia to speak at a conference. First in line at the customs counter, the official scrutinized my passport as I waited patiently. I could tell by the look on his face that there was a problem. Finally he motioned for me to step out of line. I waited and watched as each passenger filed through customs, picked up their luggage, and departed.

"Herr Thompson," a Russian officer addressed me in fluent German. "There is a problem with your visa. We are waiting for instructions from Moscow. I am sorry, I don't know how long this must take. You do understand me, yes? You do speak German?"

"Yes, I understand. What is the problem?" I asked.

"I cannot say. There should be no problem. Moscow will inform us."

I prayed and waited. I wondered how he knew that I spoke German. I was alone again with border guards, and flashed back to eight years earlier on the East German border. Now I would be preaching openly, but back then we operated in secret. So much had changed; the Wall had come down, yet these borders still felt the same. There seemed to be more freedom, but the iron hand of the KGB remained just below the surface. Another half-hour of anxious waiting and my passport was handed back to me.

"Mr. Thompson, we are sorry for the delay. Welcome to the Soviet Union."

Just like that, no explanation. I picked up my bag and joined the believers who were still waiting for me outside.

A few days after the conference, we embarked on a long drive to a small town near Odessa, on the Black Sea. An open-air evangelistic meeting was to be held there, an event that was still new and exciting to the Russian people back then. We met in the yard behind an old wooden prayer house. A little stage had been built for the speakers, and the area was filled with several hundred people. They sat on blankets the whole day listening to different guests share the Gospel.

"Jeff, it's your turn to speak," Rudy said urgently. Rudy Schepig was a Russian-German evangelist who had helped arrange the meeting.

I gazed at the expectant crowd who were waiting to hear from the only American.

"Is there a translator?" I asked. Rudy and I spoke to each other in German, but it had not dawned on him that I customarily preached in English and would need my words translated into Russian.

"Oh, that's right, you need a translator!" Rudy looked shocked. He announced from the microphone, "Is there anybody out here who speaks English?"

A schoolgirl stood up and moved forward. We shook hands as I introduced myself, and asked where she had learned English. She looked at me with a blank stare and I could see she didn't understand.

After a quick, "Please help me now, Lord," I introduced myself to the crowd. The girl struggled, and finally Rudy came over and said to me in German, "Jeff, she's not making sense."

"Rudy, she doesn't speak English." I said.

"Can't you preach in German? That way I could translate."

"Okay. Let's give it a shot. I'll do my best. But I haven't lived in Germany for seven years!"

At that moment, as I opened my mouth to speak, it was as if the Spirit of God began to fall on me and on that place. My fluency increased. Rudy looked at me. He was feeling the anointing of God's Spirit as well. There was a flow and ease of speaking in German that I didn't normally experience in English!

That evening, in that small town, God spoke to those people through Rudy and me. Over one hundred people came forward to give their lives or rededicate their lives to Christ. That was a meeting I will never forget.

EEO continued to organize various evangelistic trips. A believer from Russia encouraged me to pray for opportunities to share my faith in Christ with policemen and men in the military. Though this was not a particular interest of mine, the Lord began to bring opportunities my way.

One hot summer afternoon in Odessa, our mission team was blessed with a free afternoon. I took the opportunity to get out alone and explore the city. I jostled onto a bus, not knowing where it was going. Our translator was with the team, so I was on my own.

Holding on to the overhead rail, I noticed that a policeman was on the bus standing just a few feet away from me. I looked over at him and our eyes met. I half-nodded and smiled, and looked away.

"Lord," I thought, "Do you want me to share with this policeman?" I looked in my shirt pocket and found one small gospel tract a team member had given me the day before. Our eyes met again and we both smiled. The third time, I knew I had to do something.

I squeezed around the people standing between us, reached out my hand and looked him in the eye. "Hello. My name is Jeff." I said in Russian.

"Dmitri." he said, gesturing to himself. He waited for me to continue.

"I am from California," I said.

"Ahhh, Kahleefornyah!..." he said slowly with a smile, as if it was a dream or something he had seen on television.

At this point I had exhausted most of my Russian vocabulary. I reached in my shirt pocket and handed him the small gospel tract. "A gift," I said in Russian.

He took the tract and immediately began to read it. He didn't look up for several minutes, as if there was nothing more important at that moment than to read that booklet from front to back. I was uncomfortable, knowing that if he had questions I would not be able to answer them.

When he finished reading, he looked up at me and put the tract in his pocket. He then took my hand in two of his, squeezing my hand and shaking it at the same time.

"Thank you, Jeff. Thank you. Thank you very much." His gratefulness for the tract was remarkable. He then asked, "Jeff, do you have a Bible?"

"Biblia, Biblia," he repeated a few times to make sure I would understand. I pointed to the tract inside his shirt pocket.

"Dimitri, please, home address," I said in broken Russian. He understood, took the tract out and began writing his address on the back of it, handing it to me when he was done.

We shook hands again, and he got off the bus. Dmitri looked at me from the street, smiling, and I felt like we could have become friends. The spiritual hunger in the former Soviet Union was amazing. What I didn't know then, however, was how the Lord was going to lead me to the upper echelons of the Russian military. After all, Russia had been America's number-one enemy, and vice-versa. With my Bible smuggling past, mingling with the military and police was not a ministry goal of mine, though the Lord had other plans.

10

AN OPEN DOOR TO RUSSIAN PRISONS

Andre Ceelen, a big bearded teddy bear of a Dutchman, began campaigning for the release of "Prisoners of Conscience" in the mid-1980s. He made appointments with Russian officials to boldly inquire about the imprisonment of Christians and Russian human rights activists. Andre's informed and incessant badgering of Soviet bureaucrats, putting public pressure on them by using the European media, was pivotal in the release of men and women who had been unjustly imprisoned, such as Anatoli Scharansky, the famous Jewish dissident who is now in the Israeli Parliament.

Andre and I were friends. One day he called me from his home in Holland, "Jeff, I just got back from Russia. I have a special request from the director at the Russian Red Cross. The Prison Division of the Ministry of the Interior is requesting food to help feed young people in their youth prison system. Do you think you could find churches to help with this? If your answer is yes, I will fax you the letter."

"Sure, go ahead and fax it to me. I can't promise anything

right now, of course, but I will pray about it," I said. "Andre," I asked, "why do you think American churches would want to feed prisoners in Russia?"

"Because it's a great opportunity to help in the name of Jesus Christ. Don't you agree?"

Andre was right. I understood the need, but I was always seeking the possibility of sharing our faith, and not just offering help because help was needed. Our resources were limited, thus it was my desire to focus on projects that allowed us to share our faith as well as offer aid. When the fax arrived there was something that clicked inside my heart.

"Their youth prison system," I wondered out loud. "What is that?" I looked out over the parking lot from our newly rented office over a pizza parlor. I didn't hear any audible voices, but I sensed this was something we should help with. With the breakup of the Soviet Union, the centralized control of the economy was broken as well. Food lines at stores were common, yet it was these conditions that offered opportunities for us to share the gospel of Jesus Christ. I had many questions about this request, and responded with a page of questions which I faxed back.

Andre made an appointment for me to meet the president of the Russian Red Cross, whose name was Yuri Zapadalov. So, in December 1991, I boarded a plane to meet Zapadalov and two colonels from the Russian Ministry of Interior (MVD). The MVD was a branch of the large Russian military establishment, and was responsible for border troops, prisons, and the police.

Our meeting took place in Mr. Zapadalov's office, a small room with heavy burgundy curtains and a larger-than-life painting of Lenin smiling down on everyone. Everyone except me smoked, and the fumes hung oppressively in the air, creating a lazy haze against the Soviet red walls. I introduced myself as we shook hands. No pleasantries were exchanged, and nobody smiled except Lenin. Nobody offered any small talk. Silently I prayed. I somehow had expected a warmer, friendlier reception.

"How can we help you?" Mr. Zapadalov said in a matter-of-fact voice, opening the conversation.

I took a deep breath. The two colonels just stared at me with no expression. I was the first member of the enemy they had ever met.

I said, "Well, I received your fax. I wanted to talk about it."

"Yes. Go ahead," Mr. Zapadalov said.

"I received your request for food and I think we can help you," I said. "We can definitely help you with food. I don't know if you received my list of questions, but once we know how many prisons there are and where they are located, then we'll be able to develop a plan. We have concerns about how the food will be distributed—questions about shipping and verification that it will be delivered. We see ourselves as partners with you in meeting these needs. We will need full access to verify that the food shipments are indeed delivered to each prison. This is a primary condition of our agreement to help."

They were attentive and discussed this point of verification and providing access to the prisons. What was on my heart, however, was to offer spiritual food for the prisoners.

"We can help you with food for the body, but we would like to help you with another need as well—food for the soul."

They looked at me attentively, yet seemed puzzled.

"I would like to propose a type of spiritual rehabilitation program for your youth prisons. It would be based on biblical principles of ethics and morals that would help them in their daily lives."

There was a long silence. I was uncomfortable and felt very out of place. It had only been 20 months since I had been allowed into Russia, much less proposing an idea to cooperate with the same police who had denied me entry for so many years. Yet, this proposal was the real reason why I was sitting in that Moscow office.

Finally, one of the colonels said, "Okay, please give us your proposal."

I continued to share my thoughts about how we could help, though nothing was written on paper.

When the meeting was over one of the colonels handed me a letter. He said, "Here are the answers to your questions."

I opened the envelope, and there was a typewritten list of all 59 youth prisons in the new Russian Federation. The document was the answer to my faxed list of questions, including every prison address, telephone number, and name of the prison director, his assistant, prison population, ages of inmates, and how many beds in each prison. I found out later that this information was considered secret, and they had never given this information out before. At the same time, they were going to consider my proposal, and pass it along to their superiors.

I left the Red Cross office that day and took the metro back to the Railway Institute dormitory where I was staying with my good friend, George Bryson of Calvary Chapel. A few days later George and I got to baptize 11 brand-new believers in the Rossiya Hotel swimming pool, which marked the beginning of the first Moscow Calvary Chapel.

I bought a map of Russia. I highlighted each city with a youth prison—including those in Siberia, the Russian Far East, and the Urals—and began to analyze how we could distribute food to all these prisons. The task seemed impossible, yet exciting.

After Christmas, I sent a fax saying I would like to have a follow-up meeting, and, with their agreement, that we would like to visit some prisons and begin the rehabilitation program. In January, EEO sent a newsletter saying that we were going to take a team to preach in Russian prisons.

Seventeen people signed up for that team and in April 1992 we left for Moscow and Russian youth prisons.

There was a problem, however. The Russian government did not know we were coming! I did not have permission to actually go into the prisons yet. Mr. Zapadalov had not answered any of my faxes and his silence was something I had not expected.

As each day passed, I thought I would receive a fax from Moscow. People began to sign up and plane tickets were being purchased. At our previous meeting in December, I had said I would return in April. With no response, however, I didn't know if my requests for information had been passed on to the Ministry of Interior or not. When people signed up to go, I shared with them that we didn't know whether or not we would actually be allowed into the prisons, that we were going on faith.

Upon arrival in Moscow, our translator called the Red Cross office and left messages. On the third day, I decided to go to the Red Cross office to try to see the director myself. I figured he couldn't avoid me if I just showed up. As I turned the handle of the door to walk in from the street, I literally bumped into Mr. Zapadalov, who was on his way out. With surprise and embarrassment on his face, he accompanied me into his office and gave me the telephone number and name of the officer I should ask for at the Ministry of Interior. That was it. No small talk, no explanation.

The next day I called the Ministry of Interior and got Mr. Kleftsov. "We have been expecting your call. Why haven't you called earlier?" he asked.

"I just now received your number from the Red Cross," I said.

"When can you come and meet?"

"Anytime," I replied.

"Good. I will arrange a meeting for today at three o'clock."

Again, it was time to pray. Our team was evangelizing on the streets in Moscow while I was trying to make contact with the officials, but we had our hearts set on ministering to the young prisoners. Three o'clock came quickly.

Nervously I climbed the stairs of the three-story building with my translator. An officer greeted us and led me into a large, well-appointed office. At the conference table, sitting erect and in uniform, were eleven colonels and officers from the Ministry of Interior. I felt like a lamb being led to the slaughter. I had no idea this was to be such a high-level meeting—the chairman of the entire Russian prison system was there, with all the men who were in charge of the various regions and departments, including the colonel over the 59 youth prisons. I was there with only my translator, and it was time to get started.

Yuri Ivanovich Kalinin, the prison department chairman and who is today the Vice Minister of Justice, sat at the head of the long conference table. Not knowing what prior information they had, if any, I started from the beginning. I shared from the heart that we had more to offer than just food, but also food for the soul; a spiritual rehabilitation program for their youth prisons.

Mr. Kalinin was warm, articulate, and friendly. My previous proposal had already been discussed and he then asked me, "Well, Mr. Thompson, when would you like to implement this program?"

He had no idea that we had a team waiting and praying for this very moment. "If it is possible sir, this week. I have brought a group with me from America," I said.

He looked me in the eye, as if to determine whether I could be trusted or not, then glanced at the director for the youth prisons, Alexander Nikolayevich Dolgich, and said, "Colonel Dolgich, what do you think?"

Dolgich said, "Well, it should be possible... what's the plan?"

Because I had plotted out all the youth prisons on the map at home, I knew which youth prisons were closest to Moscow. I figured our team could stay in Moscow and we could make day trips to each prison. I had already worked out our travel schedule on paper and had brought it with me. This was a Tuesday, and I said, "If it is possible, on Thursday, we'd like to go to the prison in Iksha."

The chairman looked at Colonel Dolgich and he nodded, "Yes, it's possible."

Mr. Kalinin said, "OK, what else?"

"If possible, we would like to go to Mozhaisk on Friday."

The officials were looking at one another and half-smiling, taking their cue from the chairman. He smiled and said, "Mr. Thompson, what is the rest of your plan?"

Forging ahead and sensing boldness from the Lord, I figured I should just give them the whole plan I had made up in California. "If possible, on Saturday we could go to Tula, and perhaps on Sunday we could go to Kaluga."

He looked at Colonel Dolgich again, who nodded affirmatively. Finally, Chairman Kalinin responded and said, "I'll let you two work out the schedule. You have my complete approval. I would like a report at the end of this time and I want our representatives to accompany the group."

"We would like to perform small concerts and then teach the young men from the Bible. Is this acceptable?"

They all nodded their agreement.

What I didn't realize during the meeting was that these were the officials who had authority over the entire Russian Federation penal system. They had responsibility over hundreds of prisons and tens of thousands of prisoners. God had moved in a mighty way.

We all chatted after the meeting was over. Little did I know that in the next five years I would be meeting them all again under very different conditions: when there were hardships, when the Russian Orthodox Church was pressuring the Ministry of Interior to close prisons to foreigners, and for less serious times at birthday parties, or celebrations as these men rose in rank and in power.

EEO developed a track record with these men and in later years we were able to continue the ministry in Russian prisons while others were being closed out by political pressure. I had absolutely no idea at that moment that God had thrown the prison doors wide open to us, as he had done for Paul and Silas in Philippi in Acts 16. But in our case we were not getting out of prison; we were on our way in.

The room filled with shouts of "Praise the Lord!" when I reported the results of the meeting to the team. We all sensed the hand of God, but had no idea what awaited us. With awe and humility, we boarded the bus two days later for the first youth prison in Iksha, a suburb of Moscow.

Mr. Kleftsov, the deputy assistant to Colonel Dolgich, accompanied us on that first journey. A friendly man, he was unlike the officers I had met in December, and it seemed like he truly enjoyed being with us. We sang on the bus in both Russian and English, held devotions together with Russian translation, and tried to include him in our conversations.

That first meeting was a prototype of hundreds of prison meetings to come. They gathered 300 boys into the prison auditorium, all between 12-18 years of age, and guards stood quietly on the outskirts while we sang and gave testimonies of God's love. I gave a 30-minute message focusing on God's love and a relationship with Him.

These boys were very aware of their sin since they were in prison. And they knew about church. But they had not heard of this thing we call "having a personal relationship with God through His Son Jesus." Nobody in the auditorium that day had heard of being "born again." This was a new concept and one that had to be explained. About fifty boys came forward to express an interest in giving their lives to Christ that first meeting.

On the bus ride back to Moscow, Mr. Kleftsov asked if we could sing some more on the bus. He was literally joyful, beaming, perhaps because all had gone so smoothly, but also because the Lord was touching his heart. When we dropped him off in Moscow so he could catch the metro home, there were no handshakes, but only smiles and laughter followed by big bear hugs. It had been an amazing day.

The next day we picked up Alexander Nikolayevich Dolgich, the colonel over the 59 youth prisons and Kleftsov's boss. Evidently, Kleftsov had briefed him on everything, for as we sat on the bus, Dolgich said, "I understand Kleftsov had a good time with you yesterday?"

Half question, half statement, I didn't know if this was negative or positive. Our group was very sensitive to do nothing that would offend our military hosts. I felt completely unequipped to be dealing with colonels and generals in the Russian military. At the same time, however, it was evident the Holy Spirit was leading and guiding us and His presence was very real in our midst. It became apparent, however, that he thought Kleftsov should not have had a good time, but instead, should have been doing his job. Dolgich was agitated that Kleftsov had given such a glowing report of his time with us.

"Yes, he is a very nice man. He was a great help to us," I said.

"He said your group likes to sing. Let's hear them!" Dolgich commanded.

I turned to the group and told them the colonel has given the order for us to start singing. Within moments, God's presence was tangible as we began to worship. Dolgich didn't understand the words but he knew something different was happening. We sat together and talked, and I knew I liked this man. He was not anti-American, but he did have his preconceived ideas about America, our politics and our desire for world domination.

In the message that day, I spoke of mankind's need for forgiveness. Nobody could argue with this concept. Even an atheist, deep down in his heart, knew he needed forgiveness for none of us are perfect. As I challenged all those in the room, the guards, administration, and boys alike, to see if God's Word and promises are true, over 200 boys responded to the challenge. In addition, in the front row of the auditorium, stood Colonel Alexander Nikolayevich Dolgich, the highest-ranking official in the room, arm raised high, asking for forgiveness.

I didn't realize it at the moment, but this was the beginning of a spiritual revolution in the Russian youth prison system. It became Colonel Dolgich's mandate to make sure we shared this message of God's love and forgiveness with every one of the 25,000 teenage inmates in 59 youth prisons under his authority. One prison director after another desired to speak with us of spiritual things, and many of them put on wonderful dinner banquets in our honor. After all, long-time political enemies were now sharing meals and music together, and it was time to celebrate.

Alexander Nikolayevich (as I referred to Colonel Dolgich in formal Russian) arranged a follow-up meeting with Chairman Kalinin at the end of our trip. At that subsequent meeting, we signed a protocol that authorized Alexander Nikolayevich to assist us in our ministry in the prisons, including making arrangements for the distribution of food and supplies.

The next morning Alexander Nikolayevich came to pick me up at the Railway Institute dormitory. It was Sunday and I was headed home, and he insisted on taking me to the airport. "Why do you stay here?" he asked.

"It's cheaper." I said. "And I know other people who stay here as well."

He thought I should be staying in a big fancy hotel, something more appropriate to my status as the president of an American missions organization. We drove on to Moscow's Sheremeytovo-2 airport using German, English, Russian, and hands and feet to communicate. Then he startled me as he began to sing in the car—"King of kings and Lord of lords, glory, hallelujah! Jesus, Prince of peace, glory, hallelujah!"

I sang along with him, in Russian, as we headed to the airport. He was not in uniform, as it was a Sunday, and in that setting, I realized he was just like any other person who needed the love and forgiveness only Christ can give.

The experience was surreal, seemingly untrue, something I could never have imagined. Eleven days earlier, we had arrived to Moscow in faith, with no confirmation about going to prisons. The response to my phone calls and faxes had been silence. Now I had a protocol in my briefcase, and the colonel over 25,000 teenaged prisoners was driving me to the airport and we were singing Christian songs together with hearts full of joy.

Alexander Nikolayevich was already a believer in God. Our ministry had re-awakened his interest in spiritual things. Whether he became a born-again Christian that day or not, I cannot say. But I do know that he was God's appointed man for that time period in the 90s to open wide the prison doors in Russia for EEO.

We hugged at the terminal, and he asked when I was coming back. "We have a lot of work to do," he said.

11

SPIRITUAL REVOLUTION BEHIND BARBED WIRE

By 1994 we had teams ministering in prisons regularly. I was making frequent trips to inspect our deliveries of food and supplies.

Alexander Nikolayevich became a good friend. When not in the office, I called him by his Russian nickname, Sasha. He was a stickler for detail and we would plan the itinerary for each EEO mission team together. He wanted me to accompany every team, which of course wasn't possible. Gradually I introduced him to other EEO missionaries who were leading the teams, men like David LeCompte, Wes Bentley and Tom Monk. In turn, he introduced me to the other officials, making sure I knew the birthday of each and that I gave each one an appropriate gift.

He kept our relationship, and agreement, out in the open so the other generals would value our work. He scolded me when teams made mistakes, and protected me from making others.

Sasha was five-foot-eight-inches tall, in his early 50s, and was married with one daughter, Marina. He and his wife, Lidia, lived in a very modest apartment. He was a worrier and suffered from high blood pressure. He worried that our EEO teams would make cultural mistakes, and that it would damage our agreement.

He also worried about the appearance of impropriety, and was concerned about the opinions of others in the prison department who might accuse him of being too friendly with the Americans. Rumors swirled that he was personally benefiting from our relationship. From 1992 through 1998 we had unparalleled access to preach the gospel in Russian prisons, and this was all because of the man God had appointed over the youth prisons, Alexander Nikolayevich Dolgich.

One day sitting in Sasha's office, he invited me to accompany him on a short trip to the Mozhaisk prison to inspect the distribution of our food shipments.

"Do you want to go?" he asked.

"Sure, I would love to go," I replied.

"Good. It will be time for lunch soon. We'll go to the prison and then have a picnic at Borodino," he laughed and grabbed my hand, clearly pleased we could go together. His car and driver were waiting downstairs.

After the inspection, Sasha and I, the prison director, and a translator took a prison bus to the nearby historical site of Borodino Field. It was there in 1812 that Napoleon broke through the Russian line and captured Moscow for a brief time. It was also the site where Russian troops forced the Germans back after a long hard winter battle during World War II. Sasha was a historian, and loved retelling their history and the great battles fought on Russian soil.

The following October Sasha said, "There is an important meeting next week. The Ministry of Interior and the Orthodox Church are going to be exploring cooperation. I would like you to go there and speak about our cooperation and your work. General Sheriayev is the moderator. You have met him before. Just tell him I sent you."

The General was Sasha's immediate boss. They were both from the same hometown, Lipetsk, but Sheriayev's career had taken the fast track and he had become a general over all the prisons, while Sasha remained a colonel over the youth prisons.

I arrived at the conference on a chilly overcast day and wondered what I was supposed to do. Was I to just walk into the conference and tell the General I was to speak?

I later found out that Sasha had called Sheriayev, but was told there was no time available in the program for me. Sasha had sent me with the hope that they might find time for me. I also learned the conference was co-sponsored by Prison Fellowship. Here I was an outsider, an American, sort of barging in and asking to speak. It did not look good.

At the morning break, I approached General Sheriayev. I had met him only briefly at that meeting in Moscow with Chairman Kalinin two years earlier. He shook my hand warmly as he greeted me.

"Excuse me sir," I said, "but Alexander Nikolayevich asked me to come speak to you. He felt that I should speak here at the conference about the official cooperation that has existed between EEO and the MVD for the last 2½ years. He said you would understand."

Sheriayev looked perplexed. "I am sorry, Mr. Thompson, but we have a schedule. The time is already filled up." He stared at the schedule in his hand and said, "We must get started, but see me at the lunch break. Maybe I can find a little time."

I sat down and listened as each speaker spoke of what might be possible in the future. Some gave excellent theories on prisoner rehabilitation. Others spoke of their desire to help prisoners. None had any real experience in Russia.

At lunch, I found General Sheriayev. "Jeff, though you are not on the schedule, I will shorten the afternoon break and can give you 4-5 minutes at 3:45 p.m. Okay? I am sorry, but that is all I can do." While Sheriayev was apologetic, he was firm. It was a difficult situation and I felt uncomfortable. I wondered what was happening behind the scenes.

"We will now have a special guest from America, not on the schedule, who will report to us of their work in the prisons," Sheriayev announced. He glanced at me and held up four fingers, as if to say four minutes. I understood that it was my turn to give a very brief report and it had better be good, both for the sake of our future ministry, and for Sasha's relationship with his superior.

Nervously I looked out at the crowd of 200 people, mostly Orthodox priests clothed in flowing black robes and with Russian military officers. This was definitely a historic gathering to address the social issues facing Russia's youth, and an odd pair of traditional Russian institutions, the Church and the Military.

I introduced myself as the director of Eastern European Outreach from Southern California, and proceeded to list our accomplishments in the prisons up to that date. I listed the number of 40-foot shipping containers with bulk food supplies distributed; the amount of Bibles and Christian literature we had distributed; the number of meetings and spiritual seminars held; and I praised Colonel Dolgich and General Sheriayev for their cooperation and effort to assist our ministry. I closed referring to "our joint agreement, an annual protocol that we have as a partnership already in its third year with the MVD. Thank you, General Sheriayev for these few minutes to share this report."

As I stepped down from the podium, several hands shot up with questions. The general asked me to stay.

"With what church are you affiliated?" a priest asked.

I knew the religious questions would be a minefield and I asked the Lord for wisdom, "None in particular; we are an independent missionary organization supported by many different churches."

"Why don't you give your support to our Church and allow

us to distribute it? After all, these prisoners are Russian."

"Because our partnership is with the MVD and they have requested us to work with them." I answered.

General Sheriayev beamed and then asked me a question. "How many prisons have you been to, Jeff?"

"Our teams have been to 38 different prisons so far, and we have a team visiting prisons in the Tula region as we speak. I have personally been to about 30 prisons," I added.

The questions kept coming and I spent another 20 minutes elaborating on our official cooperation. The people in the room were stunned. The realization was sinking in that the MVD was serious about spiritual transformation in their prisons. The Orthodox priests in the crowd clearly weren't happy that a Western, non-Russian Orthodox organization had such access to the prison system. The staff from Prison Fellowship was shocked as well.

As I stepped down, the general winked at me, then shook my hand and said, "There is a banquet tonight at the House of Culture and I want you to be my guest. Chairman Kalinin will be there. I know he will want to see you. I will have a car and driver waiting outside and we will ride together. "

The general was clearly pleased that I would accompany him. I didn't know Sheriayev that well, but I knew that within the prison system he had a great deal of power and influence. Spending personal time with him would be good for the EEO prison ministry. Clearly, the Lord was giving me favor with these powerful men.

When Chairman Kalinin entered the banquet hall that night, General Sheriayev made sure I was seated directly across from him. Sheriayev and Kalinin sat together. I sat across from them, and the Prison Fellowship director, who hosted the dinner, sat two more chairs down. At these types of functions, protocol and seating priority are very important, and Sheriayev had changed things to fit his desires.

The food, including the caviar, was excellent. We talked and shared stories with one another. When the evening came to an end, the Prison Fellowship director invited

Chairman Kalinin to stand up and give the last toast. In classic Russian culture, stories, compliments, and heartfelt thoughts are expressed in the raising of the glass together. One would never say "cheers!" in a Russian toast. It is a much more elaborate ritual.

Kalinin stood up, raised his glass, and then asked if I would please stand up and give the last toast. It was an honor, and indicated a new level of trust and respect in our ministry to Russian prisons.

While Sheriayev and Kalinin beamed, others in the room frowned. I quickly asked the Lord for the right words to say. I stood up and spoke of our unity of purpose in seeing hope and spiritual transformation take place in our lives, the lives of prisoners, and for the Russian people.

The next morning Sasha called. "Jeff, please come by the office; there are some things to discuss."

Still basking in the smashing success of the conference and banquet, I knew that Sasha would want to hear all about it. He probably couldn't contain himself and wanted to see me as soon as possible.

"Jeff, I understand from General Sheriayev that you gave an excellent report, and that afterwards you attended the banquet as his guest. That is wonderful. However, you must know it is possible our cooperation could come to an end."

I couldn't believe my ears.

"Why, what is the problem?" I asked incredulously.

"There was a Russian on your team," he said. "An ex-prisoner, a criminal. Who is this man? Why didn't you inform us? What were you thinking?" Sasha was angry.

"Alexander Nikolayevich, that man is a Christian who has a ministry to prisoners."

"Jeff, that man is an ex-prisoner with no job, no residence permit, and no permission to be on your team. Our cooperation does not allow you to put prisoners on your team!"

By now he was raising his voice and I remained silent. He began talking directly to the translator, saying not to translate, and began explaining the problem in detail, knowing I knew enough Russian to understand him. He paced back and forth, knowing that if Sheriayev found out, our agreement could be over. It was an honest mistake on my part, and one that I didn't know I had made. Our agreement said nothing about whether or not ex-prisoners could work with EEO.

The MVD had no respect for former prisoners, of course, and to their way of thinking, an ex-prisoner had no place working with an important American organization. The hotel clerk in Lipetsk, Sasha's and Sheriayev's hometown, had refused to allow this man a bed because he did not have the proper identification. The MVD representative accompanying our group, upon their return to Moscow, had reported the incident to Sasha.

Sasha was furious because he was afraid that Sheriayev would find out. Other men in Sasha's position would not have made the effort to protect and nurture our relationship, but he was racking his brain for a solution.

"I can see that I have raised you up too quickly! Do you think that because you have dinner with Kalinin you can do whatever you want? You don't know what you are doing. Sheriayev would dismiss you in a moment if he knew about this."

"Jeff doesn't understand," Sasha said to the translator. "Sheriayev is happy when things go well, but if there is a problem, he will end this agreement and I will take the blame. He doesn't care about our cooperation. He only wants to use it to show how efficient he is."

After a two-hour tongue-lashing, I left Alexander Nikolayevich's office completely dejected. Within 24 hours, I had been highly praised by the General and totally destroyed by the Colonel. It appeared that I was now in the middle of a political dilemma for the men. Kalinin was being considered for a Cabinet position and was above the fray. But in the dark hallways of the Moscow headquarters of the MVD, I found myself asking the Lord what He was doing, and what I should do next.

I never did find out how serious that infraction really was. I always felt that part of Sasha's anger was fueled by the success of the conference and Sheriayev taking the credit, in front of Kalinin and the other generals, for the successful cooperative agreement with EEO. However, God was good, and despite our infraction, we signed another agreement with the MVD for 1995.

The Parliament, influenced by the Russian Orthodox Church, proposed a new religion law. By the summer of 1995, details emerged that this law was designed to restrict missionary work. The Orthodox Church was alarmed at the number of new churches being planted by foreign missionaries and wanted to protect their "sheep" by restricting the influx of new religions. New cults and pagan groups had made the news with their strange rituals, and this information was enough to cause Parliament, under the heavy influence of the Orthodox Church, to protect the Russian people from the evils of "non-Orthodox" religions.

My relationship with Colonel Dolgich was still strong and together we had already planned the itineraries for the EEO prison teams. Now, however, he couldn't do anything to help since it was out of his hands. "Jeff," he said, "everything may be cancelled. I cannot help you. I cannot give the final approval. General Sheriayev is on vacation so you must meet tomorrow with General Orlov."

"But Alexander Nikolayevich, this new law hasn't even been voted on yet. There is no new law. It is simply a proposal. We have an agreement," I protested.

My protests seemed in vain, however. The MVD was very

sensitive to the changing political situation, and if the Orthodox Church was going to win this battle, the MVD did not want to be found on the wrong side.

By the summer of 1995, the Russian Orthodox Church felt it was under a well-funded attack by religious groups from the West. The Orthodox Church saw the various private ministry activities as a monolithic invasion. American evangelists were now on television, school teachers were attending CoMission meetings arranged by Campus Crusade For Christ and others, and EEO was helping extensively in the prison system. New Bible-believing churches were being planted and pastored by non-Russian-speaking foreigners, and were advertising their presence on radio and in newspapers.

Russia was not ready for this type of religious freedom. The Reformation led by Martin Luther had never reached Russia so there was little understanding of the concept of individuals making a personal commitment to Jesus Christ.

The next day, as our summer teams were literally in the air, which meant over 50 people would be arriving that afternoon, I prayed while riding in the taxi to the Moscow headquarters of the MVD. Colonel Dolgich's words and demeanor caused me to be uneasy. He paced back and forth, straightened my tie, and reviewed the major points of our agreement.

"Jeff, the agreement was approved by Chairman Kalinin, so be sure to remind General Orlov of that fact. He is in uniform today, which is good. It means he is showing you respect. Good luck."

I nervously walked down the bare hallway and down the stairs to the executive offices reserved for the generals. As I was seated in General Orlov's office, I remembered that we had met on a few previous occasions.

General Orlov shook my hand. Without smiling, he pointed to the chair across from his desk. "What can I do for you?" he asked.

I sensed this meeting was to be all business. There were

no "how is life in California?"-type questions.

"General Orlov, thank you for seeing me today. Alexander Nikolayevich instructed that I should see you regarding our cooperation agreement with the MVD which was approved by Chairman Kalinin. We have teams arriving today with itineraries already planned under our agreement with the MVD, and I want to be sure there will not be any problems."

"We are the police," Orlov said, "and if this law is passed we must enforce the law. That is our job. We cannot break the law on behalf of this agreement."

"Yes sir. However, the law has not been passed yet, and our teams are not acting solely as missionaries, but as partners in our agreement. I believe we will be within the law," I said.

He looked at me and thought for a moment. I felt as if the Lord had given me just the right words to say.

"Okay, I agree, but we cannot guarantee the future of this agreement until we see this new law," General Orlov said. "Anyway, we know you, and since we have worked together well for several years everything should be okay."

I stood up. "Thank you sir." We shook hands and our 10-minute meeting was over. I thanked the Lord under my breath.

Back in Sasha's small office, I reported on our brief conversation.

"Praise the Lord!" he said when I told him of Orlov's reaction. We then lunched on cucumbers, tomatoes, and cheese while jointly breathing a sigh of relief. Sasha Dolgich had become a very good friend. He knew exactly how to work the political system of the MVD to keep our agreement intact, and to protect himself if anything went wrong.

"Alexander Nikolayevich, I have invited my father to come with me on a trip to Russia and I would like you to meet him."

"Your father? Really, when are you coming?"

"In early October."

I could see Sasha's mind racing as he thought about this.

"Do you have a schedule or plan for your father's time in Moscow?" he asked.

"No, not yet," I replied. "I wanted to ask your thoughts about it first."

"Jeff," he said, when you return in August for your trip to Siberia, I will be here. We will meet again to review the final details of your trip. Unfortunately, I will be gone for the whole month of October on a business trip."

"Alexander Nikolayevich, I am disappointed my father will not get to meet you. I have told him so much about you."

"Jeff, I cannot change it. I am very sorry, as I would love to meet your father too. Do not worry, just get me the details and I will make all of the arrangements."

With Sasha's approval and help, we planned a journey across Siberia to distribute libraries of Christian books and videos to youth prisons. Accompanying me were David LeCompte, Pastor Bob Claycamp, Hugo Holzapfel from Germany, and two translators.

The four of us carried 4,000 pounds of books. From August 15 to September 14, 1995, we became pack mules, carrying, loading, unloading and distributing the books. But there was also real joy in preaching the Gospel in this remote part of the world. It was truly an epic journey across Siberia and the Far East.

We had our first prison outreach at Angarskaya, near Irkutsk and Lake Baikal. The prison camp officials were friendly and hospitable. The darkened auditorium was filled with 350 boys from 12 to 20 years of age. Pastor Bob Claycamp, an EEO Board member, played guitar and sang, and after the message ninety percent of the boys stood and prayed to receive Jesus. Each of the boys standing in their threadbare blue cotton uniforms, shaved heads and tattoos, prayed in unison asking for forgiveness of their sins. The prison officials were both amazed and proud of their boys.

We left a complete library of 500 books at the prison. Each library consisted of complete Bibles, New Testaments, study books, biographies and an assortment of Christian videos in Russian such as "The Cross and the Switchblade." A local church group taught a Bible class in this prison and they followed up with the boys.

Our next stop was nine hours down the line, at Ulan Ude, in the Buryat Republic near the Mongolian border. The Buryat people are one of approximately 150 different ethnic groups in the former Soviet Union and Buddhism is their main religion. We were a long way from Moscow and the influence of the Colonel. The prison officials allowed us to leave the books in the boys' barracks, but did not allow them to attend a Bible study following our meeting. The spiritual atmosphere was heavy and oppressive.

The next stop, a 30-hour train ride later, was the town of Chita. A local pastor picked us up and took us to his home for a shower and nap. It was Sunday morning, and after church, we went to the high-security men's prison.

The officials were waiting for us. The prison was surrounded by 12-foot walls, barbed wire and guard towers. The barracks had been built before the Bolshevik Revolution by the Czar. The officer informed us that 150 men were waiting. The 4,000 men here were all in transition, waiting for their sentence to be determined so they could be transferred to various permanent prisons. The roomful of men was quiet, tough, and intimidating. The drawn faces of the men showed hardship and fatigue. Nobody smiled. They all wore the same ragged cotton uniform with name tags across the pocket.

Physically, we were tired from the long train ride and the hot weather. After the music and message, I challenged the men to pray with us. "The Lord requires two things of you: honesty and courage," I said. "You must be honest with yourself and with God. And you must have the courage to stand up for Jesus Christ and turn from your old way of life."

I looked at the crowd. There were no expressions, no nods of agreement; only sunken eyes staring blankly back at us. The men looked at one another uncomfortably. They shifted around in their chairs and murmured. Still nobody stood up.

"Is there even one man who will stand up for Jesus?" I asked.

A man in the front slowly stood up and smiled at me. Others in the room began to mock him. He didn't care, he had taken a stand for Jesus.

The prisoner's name was Valeri. He used to be a Christian, he said, but he had found it too hard. He wasn't sure that God would accept him since he had sinned by rejecting God previously. He told me later, "I was compelled to stand up. I know I could practice my faith privately, read the Gospels and pray. But I felt I must stand up for Jesus. I wanted to talk to you. I just wanted to talk. I was in the Communist Party. Everybody knows this. I was an officer. I had a career and a pension. I threw it all away. I left God. But today I stood up for Jesus."

Valeri knew that life would be especially harsh for him in prison from that day forward. He decided, though, that he was going to stand for Jesus. We prayed together that he might have God's supernatural strength.

On our way out of the prison, an officer told us that the prison was extremely over-crowded. "Moscow won't do anything about it," he said matter-of-factly. "Come with me."

Our destination was the high-security section of the prison. Iron doors slammed behind us in the corridor. One guard struggled with the key to open one of the windowless steel doors. The men's groaning could be heard through the door. He succeeded, allowing a little fresh air into the cell. We were not prepared for the sight. On the far wall, the cell window was boarded up. Prisoners had broken the wood and the lucky ones, or more appropriately, the strongest ones, were able to get close enough to stick their faces next to the opening for a breath of fresh air.

Seventy men occupied 300 square feet of space. A little like stuffing 70 people into your kitchen. Two bare wooden tables were covered with food, articles of clothing, and trash. You couldn't see the floor. Twelve old wooden bunk beds lined the walls. Cloth sacks hung from wire strung between the walls. Men leaned on one another because there was no room to lie down in this cell that had been built for twelve people. A bucket for human waste stood in the corner. The stench was nauseating.

The men were wearing underwear or ragged shorts. They just stared at us with empty eyes. One of the men told us to tell people what the conditions were like because it is against the law to treat people as they were being treated. These men were just trying to survive long enough to be transferred out of that hole.

We gave out some literature and talked a little about the reality of God. One older man said, "Personally, I don't believe in God. My father was put in prison during the Revolution. I received ten years in prison under Stalin for my father's crimes. I remember Christians in prison during those years. They always shared their parcels and letters with the rest of us. They should never have been put in prison."

The train stopped briefly at Nercinsk where we were to disembark. We had three minutes to get all the books unloaded. Passengers pitched in to help, and as the train departed, there we stood, next to our boxes, no train station in sight. Just some asphalt and the train track, and that was it. Eventually someone showed up to give us a ride in their small military jeep, called a Niva. Even though this was a gloomy place and our initial welcome was subdued, by the end of the day we had experienced God's blessing.

The boys in the prison were thankful for the books and the time we spent with them. Needless to say, nobody had ever been by to visit them in this remote location. We spoke at the men's prison as well. That night one of the officers prepared a meal of cucumbers, tomatoes, mashed potatoes, borscht, bread, and smoked fish. We distributed EEO tee shirts as gifts and gave the director a nice watch. They gave us hand-carved wooden boxes as a remembrance of our visit there and asked us to come back.

Our trip included stops at Birobidjan, Kharbarovsk, Vladivostok, Sakhalin Islzand, and the peninsula of Kamchatka. Sometimes the reception by prison officials was warm, at other times it was chilly. We always got cooperation, however, after we announced we had an official agreement with the Ministry of Interior signed by Chairman Kalinin, General Sheriayev, and Colonel Dolgich.

On several occasions, we learned of local Russian or American missionaries who visited the prison camps. It was great to know that follow-up teaching was available and our visit was not their only exposure to Christianity. Everyone was impressed with the variety of books in the library and we felt certain that they would be put to good use.

The response from the youthful inmates varied too—some could not be bothered to hear what we had to say, others embraced Jesus with all their hearts. We were thankful that so many were saved. We also knew that the Christian books we left behind were like acorns, and that the message of the saving power of Jesus would grow in the lives of future readers.

As we flew into Petropavlovsk-Kamchatskii, the capital of Kamchatka, the rock formations in the water and the volcanoes we saw were breathtaking. This was to be our last stop. Pastor Bob was able to share Christ with one of the colonels who was hosting us. The Colonel told Bob that he believed in God, had read the Old Testament and was reading the New Testament as well. He said he had been off vodka for two years, and had found more joy reading the Bible than he ever did in drinking vodka. Conversations like that meant so much to us; it was evidence of God working in the lives of individuals in Russia.

In October my father Jim and I landed at Moscow's Sheremeytovo airport. It was his first and only time in Russia. It was a trip he had never expected to make. For him, Russia was communist, evil, and represented everything he was against.

After a night of rest, I called the MVD headquarters and Colonel Dolgich's assistant, Vitaly Klevtsov, answered. "Where are you and when are you coming over?" he asked. "You have a meeting with General Sheriayev tomorrow at 1 p.m. We will send a car to come pick you up."

Irina, our translator from Kiev, remarked how excited they were that my father was with me in Moscow. I had learned a few years earlier how important it was to have an excellent translator who would be respected by these military men.

The black Volga four-door sedan pulled up outside our hotel, its roof-mounted blue light flashing for all to see. Vitaly stepped out and gave us hugs and handshakes. We climbed into the car and roared off, laughing and talking, without stopping at red lights. Vitaly was a jovial man, unlike many of the other officers, and was clearly happy to meet my dad. He ushered us to General Sheriayev's office door and indicated he would be waiting back in Sasha's office.

General Sheriayev, in uniform, sat at his desk. My father

couldn't believe where he was; it was like a dream. For some reason he was now meeting Russian generals, men whom he thought were the enemy.

"Welcome Jeff, come in!" Sheriayev got up and gave me a big hug. I was always nervous in his presence. I introduced my father.

"How is your time in Moscow so far?" he asked. "I have been looking forward to meeting Jeff's father. Jim, do you like to hunt? I want to invite Jeff to go bear-hunting with me. Perhaps you would like to come along?"

My dad was an avid hunter. He liked Sheriayev immediately. After 15 minutes of light talk, I presented the General with a gift in honor of his recent promotion, a beautiful leather brief case. It was almost time to go and Sheriayev stood up.

"Jeff, thank you," he said. Not to be undone, he also had a gift to give. He handed me a shiny wooden hand-carved box. I opened the box to see a gleaming 16-inch bear-hunting knife.

"You must bring this when we go bear-hunting," he laughed.

For the next three days we had a car and driver at our disposal. They pulled out all the stops to honor my father's visit by arranging tickets to the Bolshoi Theater (four seats center row ten rows from the orchestra), the Kremlin museums, the Armory, and to special dinners.

My dad's reaction? Well, he came away understanding that the Russians were people just like us. They were no longer the enemy, but instead, they were people whom he liked and respected.

By the summer of 1996, one could sense that the political climate was changing in Russia. Each year it became increasingly difficult for Colonel Sasha to push through our joint agreement. He made sure I made appearances at birthday parties for Generals Sheriayev and Orlov, and gave each one appropriate gifts. Each agreement had to be signed by Chairman Kalinin.

Sasha refused invitations to the United States to visit prisons. Prison Fellowship, however, founded by Watergate conspirator and former Nixon aide Chuck Colson, brought Chairman Kalinin over a few times to meet White House dignitaries and others. This, I believe, also indirectly helped our ministry continue in the prisons, as Kalinin remained very positive about our ministry and that of Prison Fellowship.

Where EEO was active teaching and preaching inside the prisons, Prison Fellowship worked on a political level. They also encouraged and pushed for a greater cooperation between the Orthodox Church and the Ministry of Interior.

I could see the proverbial handwriting on the wall. The Russian Orthodox Church was asserting its power, and they didn't want evangelicals on the religious scene. Our agreement lasted through the end of 1998, long after other Western groups were no longer welcome in Russian prisons.

Today, Pastor Sergei Danielenko, our EEO representative in Moscow, sits on the board of a council set up by Prison Fellowship to coordinate the ministry of churches and religious groups into prisons. Pastor Sergei is himself an ex-prisoner, and he has helped establish 34 rehabilitation centers for ex-prisoners who have confessed Christ as their savior, but have nowhere to go when released from prison.

Our prison ministry has changed, and national Russian pastors and workers now do most of it. Ironically, most of them are ex-prisoners whose lives have changed and who have found purpose by returning to the prisons to preach the gospel. Generous EEO sponsors support these men as they visit the prisons supplying Bibles, Christian literature and other supplies. I still personally minister in Russian prisons, but it is no longer on the same scale as during the days when we had an official agreement.

12
CHILDREN AT RISK

After several years of ministry in the youth prisons of Russia, I felt we had to somehow respond earlier in the life tragedy of these young people. The boys of the youth prisons told horrific stories of physical abuse, neglect, and fending for themselves on the streets.

Most of them I spoke with were "social orphans," meaning they had at least one living parent, but for their safety, they had become wards of the State. The problem of orphaned children has spiraled out of control. Most orphans come from dysfunctional families where kids run away to escape abuse. They live on the streets, sniff glue, and are eventually arrested or put into a shelter.

The EEO Child Sponsorship ministry was born as a result of working with the broken and traumatized lives of young people. I felt that if we could build a ministry to assist mothers with their children so they might experience the hope needed to raise their children and not abandon them. Since 90% of the orphan population are social orphans with at least one living parent, this meant the family unit was in crisis.

The Chernobyl nuclear accident in northern Ukraine only served to magnify the problem. If families ever lived in a state of desperation and despair, it was the families living near the nuclear plant where radiation was released into the atmosphere in 1986.

So, the Lord brought all of these things together in my mind. I had seen firsthand what happened to children in the prison system. Action was needed to keep them out of prison in the first place. The street children were already abused and only one step away from an institution. Finally, the Chernobyl victims, forgotten by their government, were left to scrounge for themselves. If they did not die from radiation poisoning, they lived with chronic illness, disease and despair.

As I prayed about these things, I asked myself what the common denominator was. It became clear that we could make a difference in the lives of children if we could help keep families together. A child raised by a single mother, or grandparent, is still much better off than being in an orphanage. If children had a roof over their heads, nutritious food, and the love of a parent, they could have a chance in life. Thus, our first goal was to intervene early enough to keep children at home by assisting parents or caregivers. A mother's arms are a perfect incubator for the gospel.

One of the incidents that touched my heart at the time was conveyed to me by Jim Hofford, a friend with a missionary heart who was a retired journalist with the *Boston*

Globe. I had asked Jim to go to Kiev to discover what was going on in the lives of the street children there. Here is the story Jim shared with me.

There were eleven of us, four adults and seven children, standing at the entrance of an old apartment house, whispering to each other. Roman, our group leader asked his assistant Tanya to keep the three youngest children with her. "We'll all go down to the basement to see what's going on," he told her. "Just keep a close watch, OK?"

She nodded, and Roman led the way to the apartment building basement.

We descended wet concrete steps into absolute darkness. Roman turned on his flashlight. After 5-6 steps, I could see a large iron gate ahead. Roman pushed it open and it responded with a long creak of complaint. We all passed through in single file. The smell of urine and feces filled our nostrils.

We stepped through a small opening into the basement proper. As our flashlights probed the darkness, I could see a room that was perhaps 20 feet square. It was filled with old paint cans, rocks, newspapers, ripped plastic bags, broken glass, and had a museum supply of water pipes overhead. The floor was dirt.

At the far corner of the room we could see a doorway. Roman and his children approached it very slowly, their flashlights searching the floor every step of the way. We could see them enter the room... and then almost instantly there were screams and yells, and a chattering of excited voices. Mingled with the excited chatter were shouts of, "We found them. We found them! In here!"

Our evening's safari had been a success. We had just "captured" eight of the most precious, endangered creatures on the face of this planet. Our flashlights illuminated eight orphan children who were crouching, sitting, lying on piles of old cardboard and newspapers, their eyes blinking against the light. I wasn't ready for this. I could only stare and try to hold back the tears. It was a surrealistic nightmare scene exceeding anything from the stage of *Les Miserables*.

The eight forsaken children were filthy, pale, and fearful. Roman and the children with us reassured them. We're here to help you! We're your friends! We have food and drinks!"

"How long have you been here?" I asked the newly discovered orphans. Four of them had been there only a few nights, two others for a week, one for nearly two weeks.

"Why did you leave home?" I asked.

Their stories were all too common. "Because I couldn't live at home anymore... I was afraid... I didn't want to be beaten ... there were guys at home beating each other ... my father doesn't want me anymore."

Of all my brief conversations with the children, I can never forget one in particular. There was a seven year old blonde-haired girl next to a concrete wall, lying on flattened sheets of cardboard. I remember kneeling down to her and asking her name.

"Anastasia," she whispered.

Her blue eyes were subdued, her hair matted, but there was a hint of a smile on her face. I touched her shoulder very gently.

"Anastasia, God loves you and I love you."

She smiled the most fragile smile I have ever seen ... the smile of an angel ... and closed her eyes slowly.

"Thank you," she murmured in Russian.

At that moment, Roman opened a large shopping bag full of food for the children... some chunks of sausage, rolls, some Fruit Loops cereal and a large bottle of Sprite with plastic cups. The food was all passed around.

About 30 minutes later we all headed out of the basement dungeon. As we did, I felt a small tug on my sleeve, and looked down. It was little Anastasia, looking up at me with a radiant smile, and holding out her hand to give me something. "What's this?" I asked in great surprise.

"For you," she nodded. She gave me a handful of her Fruit Loops cereal and was gone, scurrying away with the other children and Roma the orphanage director. As they crossed the street to go start a new life, Anastasia looked back, waved, and said, "*Dasvedanya*"—goodbye. It was an experience I will never forget.

I met Irina and Yuri Skrypnik in Kiev in 1992 through a mutual friend, Larissa Lange. Larissa, after working for us for two years as a translator, had become a Christian during our early prison ministry. She decided to emmigrate to Canada, but before she left she said, "You're going to need someone to take my position to be chief translator. I have a good friend who can do the job. I'd like to recommend her."

We had helped plant the first Calvary Chapel in Kiev, and Irina and Yuri began attending that church shortly after they were saved. I was privileged to have baptized Larissa, Irina and Yuri in a little swimming pool at a school on a Sunday afternoon in Kiev in 1993.

When Larissa departed, Irina left her teaching position at the University in Kiev and joined EEO. She immediately began the process of incorporating EEO Ukraine as an international charity fund, not as a religious organization. The Ukrainian government's attitude toward foreign religious groups was not positive, and we desired to stay clear of that minefield.

We started small. Our goal was not to fix the families that were broken, but to somehow help preempt the process. We began visiting families in the radiation-contaminated region of Ukraine in late 1994. We decided God wanted us to help support 50 families, without having any sponsors lined up. It was a real step of faith. We visited families, got their information, and investigated their situations.

As the number of families grew, Irina gathered others around her to help. Her husband Yuri and others joined the ministry. Coordinators (caseworkers) were needed to supervise the child sponsorship ministry. The EEO ministry in Ukraine, managed admirably by Irina, is staffed by Ukrainian Christians. Together we partner with EEO sponsors in America to see the lives of at-risk children and their families changed by the gospel of Jesus Christ.

One of our early coordinators was Nina Sulimova. Nina was actually being accepted into the child sponsorship program because her husband had abandoned her with two children to raise. A fire in her apartment had left the family with nothing. When Irina first approached Nina it was to ask about needy families in Nina's church. As she sat in Nina's apartment, the walls still blackened by the recent fire, Irina said, "Nina, we need to accept you into the program first."

Nina loved the Lord. She assumed receiving support also meant she had a job to do. She has now been a coordinator for many years and loves the families in her care. Many of her families have found jobs and graduated out of the program.

The chain reaction of faith continued in the life of Nina's son Dima. When Irina first visited that smoke-blackened apartment, Nina and her son Dima slept on a mattress on the floor. Dima was 13 years-old and bitter because his father had left the family. When Dima was invited to the very first EEO Bible camp he refused to go. He did attend the second year, however, but still did not ask the Lord into his life.

Another year went by, but still he did not open himself to the Lord.

Dima was shy and angry, but Christian friends began to encourage him. Eventually he was saved through the ministry of Calvary Chapel, Kiev and was transformed by the grace of God. Dima grew in the Lord and went from being a camp attendee to a camp counselor. Each summer as EEO teams returned, team members would marvel at how Dima was growing in his faith.

In one of our meetings, Dima politely asked if he could speak to the crowd. The team had traveled to a village church and Dima had come along to help. "Dima, do you know what you want to say?" the team leader asked.

"Yes, I have been praying about this for a while. I know exactly what I want to say."

Dima stood up in front of the 300 people in the church. He began to recite a poem. It wasn't just a simple couple of lines, it was a five-minute poem recited from memory.

Our visiting American team stood there with him on the platform. They watched as people began to cry. In his poem, Dima was pleading for people to give their hearts to Jesus Christ. This shy young boy, whom we had met several years earlier living in a charred apartment, dealing with the baggage of a father who had abandoned him, was now boldly imploring people to give their lives to Christ. His life is a picture of restoration and a testimony to the power of God and sponsorship. Today, Dima attends college and would like to go into full-time ministry.

We have many other coordinators on the frontline of service with at-risk children, and I have great admiration for them. One of these coordinators is Valentina Shvets, who has a deep love for all the families she serves. She recently shared a story with me about a girl named Yana. It is a wonderful example of what is happening among families who are in the EEO program.

Yana started to attend Sunday school at a local Bible-believing church in Kiev. Yana's mother Natalya, who had been raised in the Ukrainian Orthodox Church, and was unsure of the teaching her daughter was receiving, wanted to forbid her daughter from attending those classes. But once at night she heard the voice that tenderly told her not to forbid her child from going there. It was immediately understood that the Lord Himself was talking to Natalya, because of the love she heard in that voice.

Back then the family lived in sin and in poverty. But by Yana's prayers, her mother came to the Lord in 1996, repented and was baptized in the church her daughter attended.

The following year her father repented and was baptized too. He was also set free from alcohol addiction, and started earning good money. The life of the family was completely changed. God restored the relationship between the parents. They started loving each other, praying all the time, reading the Word of God, and doing their best to help others in need.

The most zealous of three of them was the father. He woke up at 4 a.m. every day to pray and read the Word. He witnessed to people all the time, shared how God had changed his life, and was very thankful to the Lord.

Exactly one year later, in 1999, during worship at church, God called Yana's father to Himself. The doctors' diagnosis was cardiac arrest.

By that time the mother, Natalya, had had two very serious operations and didn't have a job. Yana's mother didn't have any relatives, and her husband's relatives said that they wanted to see how God would help Natalya and her daughter survive.

God is not mocked. Natalya found a job, even though it was very difficult. Instead of working in a school—Natasha was a Russian-language teacher—she took a job as a store assistant selling soap. At that same time Eastern European Outreach accepted Yana into its care.

It was an indisputable testimony to all relatives and acquaintances that God exists! Every month Yana's little family started to receive money from EEO. Thanks to the money, Yana was able to go to a good grammar school where she could study the English language. Her dream came true, as she wanted to be fluent in English.

After the grammar school, Yana entered a community college and hopes to attend T.G. Shevchenko University—the best-known liberal arts university in the country—to continue studying. She is a good student and is fluent in English. She is now able to help as a translator when there are foreign guests at church. Yana is dreaming of missionary work and takes part in the Youth Evangelism Ministry.

In Summer 2004 Yana successfully passed the exam to enter the University. Unfortunately, her mother didn't have money to pay for her education there. But God again intervened in such an insoluble problem. EEO had decided to help children who had grown up and who were exiting the Sponsorship Program and Yana was selected to participate.

Even though the number is always growing, there are now over 750 families and 1,200 children receiving sponsorship support in Ukraine and Russia, and 200 more children in Kosovo. We constantly seek effective ways to disciple people in their faith in Jesus Christ, and to meet needs without creating an attitude of dependency in the recipient family.

It has been exhilarating to see the Lord putting so many elements together to shape EEO. God was using the building blocks of the past to create a whole new direction for us. We are committed to the long-term solution to people's problems, which is helping them discover a personal relationship with Jesus Christ and living for Him. At the same time, we desire to empower the sponsor so that every dollar they give is used to impact an at-risk life with the grace of God.

13
THE BALKANS: TRAGEDY IN KOSOVO

It is difficult to write about our ministry in Kosovo and the Balkans without delving into a little history. Everyone who has studied the Balkans has an opinion about who is right and who is wrong. It is not my intent to give an opinion about whether or not the Kosovar Albanians have a right to the land or not. My desire is to illustrate how I feel the Lord led me there and how He directed our steps.

Not many people know where the Balkans are or where Kosovo is in particular. Christians who read their New Testament know about Macedonia and the church in Thessalonica. This region, the northern part of Greece, continuing north through former Yugoslavia, up to Hungary, and over to Albania, Romania and Bulgaria make up what we call the Balkans.

The Balkans were dominated by the Turks during the Ottoman Empire for over 500 years, but today it is a melting pot of the world's major religions. Eastern Orthodoxy, Roman Catholicism, and Islam all collide in this churning region of ethnic violence. Stated differently, this is where three empires intersect: the Ottoman Empire (Muslim Turks); the Byzantine Empire (Eastern Christians); and the Roman Empire (Western Christians).

Albania once had a proud Christian heritage. The apostle Paul visited them to share the Gospel in the first decades of the faith. Albania was then the Roman province of Illyricum that is mentioned in Romans 15:19. However, the Turks, who led the Ottoman Empire, conquered the region in 1389 in a fierce battle on the Plains of Kosovo. As a result, the Albanians adopted the Muslim religion but the Serbians did not. It is best to make a clear distinction at this point— Albanians are moderate or secularized Muslims, very unlike those in today's Middle East.

Fast-forward to 1998 and the Serbian ruler at the time, Slobodan Milosevic. After failed campaigns to establish the dominance of Greater Serbia in Croatia and Bosnia, Milosevic turned his attention to Kosovo. Tensions were on the rise and para-military units from both sides were clandestinely killing each other. Out of this cauldron of hate came great human suffering. During the early winter of 1999 the Serbian army made its final move into Kosovo to once and for all ethnically cleanse this cherished Serbian region and force two million Kosovar Albanians out of the area.

By mid-April 1999, over 700,000 Kosovar refugees were forced out of their homes into neighboring Macedonia, Albania, or into the surrounding mountains. Our EEO missionaries in Tirana, Albania—Bob and Eva Durham—were helping Kosovar refugee families, and were overwhelmed by the needs they saw.

In an effort to determine firsthand how EEO could help more effectively, Pastor Kevin Doyle and I, along with a work group from his church, traveled to Tirana.

In assessing the situation we went to the Tirana Sports

Palace. It was actually a run-down gymnasium with a concrete floor. It had become the new home for 3,000 Kosovar refugees who were sitting on wall-to-wall blankets. Each family had their own blanket.

Ramsia and Shevria, sisters who had married brothers, had been there for a month already. Ramsia's five children were listless and were huddled around mom. A lack of toilet and bathing facilities contributed to the severe stench of human flesh packed into the gymnasium in hot weather. Kevin and I sat down on their blanket and listened as Ramsia told us their story.

"Our husbands are still somewhere in the hills. We haven't heard anything about them since the night they started shelling our little village over a month ago."

Ramsia began to cry and continued, "When the Serbian troops came one of them grabbed my five-year-old son, Gentrit. I screamed and grabbed him right back. The soldier demanded 200 German marks (about $100), took his gun out, and laughed. We were so scared. Somebody paid this money for me. We walked 75 kilometers over hills and valleys to the Albanian border town of Kukes. From there, a refugee transport brought us to Tirana and this gymnasium." She looked at her children and put her head down, lost in her thoughts.

The first order of business was to get the two women, their children and the grandparents out of that horrible gymnasium. We found an apartment for them and in a matter of days had helped provide a little dignity to this grieving family.

Churches in Tirana were supplying bread to refugee families, and sharing the love of Christ with them in both word and deed. Just ten years before Albania had been an atheistic nation, and now they were evangelizing their ethnic cousins. I marveled at how the Lord had opened the door for the gospel to the Kosovar people.

After ten days in Tirana, helping hundreds of refugee families, we returned to the United States determined to help further. My wife Paula and I, along with another couple, Brad and Debbie Warren, were not able to return until July 2nd. The war had ended a week earlier, on June 24, 1999. The air war against Serbia lasted 78 days and resulted in a cease-fire between the warring factions. The U.N. moved troops in to keep the peace and today Kosovo, like Bosnia, is governed by the U.N.

Paula and I met with the Durhams to review how they had been helping the refugees in our absence. Eva Durham said, "Jeff, the Begajs returned to Kosovo a few days ago. One of their brothers located them, came here to Tirana, and they all took the bus back. However, they left their address in case we wanted to come visit." Eva handed me a piece of paper.

I looked at the paper. There was one word, "Banje." This was the name of their village, which didn't appear on any maps. Ramsia left instructions for us to find the town of Malisheve, and once we did, to ask there how to find Banje. In her mind, I am sure this type of navigation seemed normal, but for me, it served to increase my apprehension about entering a war zone while not knowing exactly where we were going.

My partner Brad and I filled our rented van with food, blankets, and clothing. Our driver, a local Albanian, spoke little English but had driven the treacherous road to Kosovo before. With the word "Banje" in my pocket, Brad and I said goodbye to our wives and headed for Kosovo.

The poorly paved roads of Albania were crowded with determined refugees navigating the potholes as they streamed back to their homeland. Buses, vans and tractors pulling open flatbed trailers filled the narrow mountainous road leading eastward.

Our refugee caravan came to a stop after eight torturous hours crawling over the mountains of Albania. "Excuse me, but what are the soldiers doing there? Why are we being detained?" I asked a British soldier.

"They are removing land mines, sir, planted along the

road you are traveling. I suggest sir that you do not leave the road, do not drive on the shoulder, and do not go out on the dirt roads into the villages. We have reports of thousands of small landmines," he said in a crisp formal tone. A few moments later we heard explosions as two landmines were detonated.

We followed a U.N. convoy past the long line of refugees and crossed over to Kosovo, arriving at Prizren about 6 p.m. that evening. We had been on the road for 14 hours.

"Where are we going to stay?" the driver asked in broken English. Hotels and businesses were not open. Shop windows were destroyed, buildings burned, and there was no electricity in the city. Actually, we later discovered there was no electricity in the entire country.

A German missionary friend in Tirana, Hans, had given me an address in Prizren, a southern Kosovo town, and we agreed to try to meet there later that week. I felt that we should go there and see if we could help them. As it turned out, we found the address and the home was owned by a woman, Mrs. Qafleshi, and it was the only house on her street that had not been destroyed by the Serbian army. Upon learning we were Americans, she insisted we sleep there.

A young man down the street named Jakup came over to translate for us. He implored us to come with him to meet his father and have tea with his family.

We followed him and saw a U.N.-issue refugee tent was set up on the grass in front of what used to be their family home. Three families had lived in a nice two-story home, which was now only ashes and rubble. Their only crime had been to be ethnic Albanian.

Jakup's father was thrilled to see us. He related the great losses his family had suffered and told us in detail about the great suffering that all Kosovars had experienced.

Several neighborhood children followed us to Jakup's house, hoping to hear Brad play the guitar he carried. The kids sang along and had a favorite song they wanted to sing. On that warm July evening, we sat outside by the moonlight, surrounded by destruction, and sang of freedom.

Although we've had pain,
Although we've been suffering,
Although we've experienced death,
We now have freedom,
You are free Kosova
We can be free.

"You've done so much for us," Jakup's father said when the children left that night.

I said, "No, we feel so deeply for you. We're here to help, but we really haven't done anything yet, although we'd like to."

"You Americans don't know how much you have done for us," he replied. "Just today, you brought music back into our lives. Our children can sing again. The past 10 years we've been under heavy oppression from the Serbian police. We couldn't go out after dark unless we had a reason. Many of us watched our homes, and our dreams, burn to the ground. We could not sing songs about Kosovo. Our children could not study in college. We could not drive without paying bribes to police. But tonight you have brought children into my yard to sing, and I thank you for that. You have done so much for us."

Humbled and tired, Brad, Jakup and I walked back to the Qafleshi home. I asked Jakup if he would like to work with us for a few days. "Jakup," I asked, "do you happen to know where Malisheve or Banje is?"

"I know where Malisheve is, but I don't know about Banje. No problem, we will find it tomorrow!" he said with confidence.

Late that night machine gun fire sprayed into the sky outside our gate. I dove out of bed onto the floor, our window open to the courtyard and street below. I thought we were under attack from a sniper. After a fitful night of rest, we learned in the morning the weapons had been fired by celebrating Kosovar soldiers.

The next day we departed for Malisheve with Jakup as our guide. We had been on the road about ten minutes when we came upon some people and a soldier on a hillside next to the road. We got out and found pieces of clothing half-buried in lumpy ground. The locals said it was a mass grave.

One man said in German, "Serbian troops came through this village and had forced everyone out of their homes. Women and children were forced down one road and men brought here. They had to dig their own graves and then were shot. I lost nine family members. My uncles are buried here."

We crossed the road and walked over to what used to be his home. Amid the rubble were fifteen bullet holes in the brick wall of the charred kitchen. "This is where they shot my family," he said, pointing at the wall. A blackened skull and bones lay nearby. Half a driver's license lay under the waste. We left some food for him and his neighbors, and after praying together said our goodbyes.

Finally we reached Malisheve and we discovered about eighty percent of the town had been destroyed. Every building was charred and blackened. Major fighting had taken place in the area because the Malisheve region was a stronghold of the Kosovo Liberation Army (KLA).

Jakup asked for directions to Banje, and we found it was just a few miles up the road. "Go to the NATO tank parked on the road and turn right. That will be in Banje!" the man said.

LEAVING THE AMERICAN SECTOR

I thought about the warning by the British soldier about landmines, but also observed that other vehicles drove down the dirt road with no problem, so we turned right and drove a few miles into the countryside.

When we reached the outskirts of the village we stopped to ask directions to the house. "Excuse me, do you know where the Begaj family lives?" Jakup asked.

"Which one?" There are many Begaj families here."

"Isuf Begaj," I said.

"Oh, Isuf. Go to the end of the road; that will be his house," the man said. We thanked him and gave him some chocolate for his children.

Isuf is Albanian for Joseph. I had never met Isuf, only his wife Ramsia, his father Iliaz, and his five children. He and his brother had been in the mountains the entire three months of the war. We pulled up to the gate of a house, but they were all clustered together and I wasn't sure if we were at the right place.

A man walked out. When he saw me enter the gate, he paused. Although we had never met, he recognized me from a photograph. "Americans! Americans! Jeff!" he shouted.

He yelled inside the house, and soon the entire clan rushed out to greet us. Ramsia, her sister Shevria, the grandparents, and all the children flooded out of the house. The kids ran with their arms outstretched and Ramsia cried. We all hugged and cried in one big circle in the dirt of their courtyard. Isuf slapped me on the back and hugged me. We could never have imagined this day when we all sat on the gymnasium floor in Tirana.

Jakup and Isuf became our co-workers in Kosovo, assisting us in every area. Isuf's home had been damaged but not destroyed, and it became our base of operations for providing relief to Kosovar families.

THE BALKANS: TRAGEDY IN KOSOVO

We quickly learned that if you called yourself a Christian it was like calling yourself a Serbian. The Serbian religion is Eastern Orthodox Christianity and Kosovars did not understand that one could be a Christian without being Orthodox.

We became good listeners, and shared Christ's love with the widows and orphans through our actions. We used words when appropriate.

Isuf, Jakup and I walked through many villages determining who needed help. We focused on the widows and the poorer families. One man, Rramin Krasniqi, was simply grateful that someone would take the time to listen to him. We sat on small plastic seats in front of his tent in the village of Hoce Vogel as he shared the story of the suffering he had endured.

He started with words of appreciation. "Thank you for your help. You know, I have never needed help from anyone before. My sons have worked with me in the fields and we could always take care of ourselves. Do you know what happened to us?" Mr. Krasniqi looked down, lost in his thoughts, and continued without waiting for an answer.

"Late the night of March 25th I heard people running and yelling that the Serbs were coming. I told my son Valon to take his mother and brother in the car right away, and I would stay with the house. I wanted to get supplies ready and set our cows free. At 5 a.m. that morning, I heard screaming and troops opened fire on our homes. Five old men began waving white flags, to show that there were no KLA fighters in our village. The troops forced everyone out of their homes and into the road. The wounded were shot to death.

"They told us to leave the country and never come back. About 150 of us began walking down the road towards Albania with soldiers firing their guns in the air and pulling women out of the crowd. We walked all day, the crowd getting bigger all the time. There were hundreds of us by nightfall and we stopped in an abandoned village and entered homes. The women and children wanted to sleep while we stood guard outside in the fields.

"Many of the Serbian soldiers didn't wear uniforms. They were really just regular people from the neighboring Serb villages. I recognized two of the boys because they had played with my son. They forced us into the houses. I found my family hiding in one of the houses. They made us men strip naked and stole all of our money. They said to go to sleep, that nobody would hurt us.

"My son Valon was 16 and wanted to sleep outside in the car with his friends. People were sleeping everywhere, in cars and in the fields. At 1:30 a.m. my wife woke up and checked on Valon who was sleeping in our car. At 1:45 she heard aircraft but I was sleeping. The next thing I knew, I woke up covered in concrete and broken glass. The Serbs were bombing us as we slept. I pushed the rubble off, checked on my wife, and tried to go down the stairs, except they were gone. I jumped down from the 2nd floor onto the broken concrete slab. I ran to the car and saw Valon."

"Daddy, are we still alive?" he asked me.

"Son, yes, we are all alive. How are you?"

"Dad, I am okay I think, but my arms and legs feel dead."

"The door was jammed and when I reached in the broken window to try and pull him out, his arms were only hanging by threads of flesh. I tried to tie up his arms to stop bleeding, but I couldn't."

Rramin wiped his eyes and continued.

"Valon, I can't open the door."

"That's okay Dad." he said. "Be strong, and tell Mom I love her... say goodbye for me...."

Warriors and scholars continue to debate the rightness of one side or the other in the Serb-Kosovo conflict. Each side contends that the other was acting illegally, that the opposing side was responsible for more atrocities than the other. Some even think the NATO intervention was the most brutal act of all.

I was drawn into this debate most recently in the summer of 2004 when an article by Dr. Paul Mojzes, professor of Religious Studies at Rosemont College in Rosemont, Pennsylvania, appeared in the influential *East-West Church and Ministry Report*.

Professor Mojzes presented what I felt was a rather unbalanced view of events in Kosovo, focusing only on the destruction of churches and holy places in Kosovo by ethnic Albanians, but almost completely ignoring the fact that many of these acts were retribution against Serbians who had committed atrocities against Kosovars in the name of Christ.

Of course, there was no justification for the violence on either side, but it troubled me that Dr. Mojzens, like so many other Christians, had taken sides in the conflict, and I felt it was perhaps politically motivated.

The one factor that has always concerned me was that Serbians consider themselves Christians, yet they were responsible for some pretty diabolical acts in the name of Christ.

As you might imagine, this made it difficult for us to minister to the Muslims of Kosovo. We came in the name of Christ too, and they thought we might kill them. It took hard work and prayers to build trust with the Kosovar Muslims before we could minister to them. We had to explain that as evangelical Christians, we were very different from the members of the Serbian Orthodox Church that had been slaughtering their families. Thankfully, there were many Kosovar Muslims that could look beyond the politics to see the love and mercy of Jesus Christ, and they embraced the Lord as a result.

Dr. Mark Elliott, editor of *East-West Church and Ministry Report*, printed my concerns, and that seemed to generate more heat than light. In my letter, I said, "...one definitely detects a pro-Serbian slant to every single issue [Dr. Mojzes] mentioned.... I would hope that the *East-West Church and Ministry Report* would either stay out of partisan politics, or at least provide opposing viewpoints."

Sadly, my call for a balanced perspective fell on deaf ears. Many Christians feel a need to be on the "right" side of an argument, forgetting there are souls at stake, not just ideologies.

Through the dedication of sponsors we have been able to help many families in Kosovo. Isuf Begaj still works with us part-time. Jakup worked with us for several years and now works in Prizren. He has three beautiful children and Isuf and Ramsia now have six. In many ways, life has returned to normal except for the ethnic tension, which is always just under the surface.

Our friends, Randy and Lycia Harvey, went to Kosovo as EEO missionaries and have started a growing church in Malisheve, so the seeds of our ministry continue to produce fruit. We also provide food to poverty-stricken familes there.

The work of evangelism is a tough one in Kosovo. With a largely Muslim population, most people are reluctant to leave the religion of their fathers and grandfathers. It takes time to build trust and friendships in this part of the world.

At EEO, we continue to remember the widow and the orphan, to reach out to the poor and needy. We pray that all of our labor is contributing to the building up of the Body of Christ in Kosovo.

One night as I prayed in a circle, holding hands with six widowed mothers and their 19 children, I thought of Psalm 68. The Scripture says: "A father of the fatherless and a defender of the widow, is God in His holy habitation."

I prayed, "Lord, we ask that you would be a father to these children and a defender of these widows. And if you are calling us to be that line of defense for them, Lord, we want to be in obedience to Your Word. Please make Your presence, and Your love, real to these children and their mothers."

God has called EEO to remember the poor, the widow, and the orphan in Kosovo. To remember them means to defend them. To defend them means to care for them. We will continue to do so as long as He leads us to do so.

14
A CHANGING
OF THE GUARD

The person who said, "The only constant thing in life is change," was right on target. In the 90s EEO ministry was largely focused on evangelizing in Russian prisons. Simultaneously we expanded to help at-risk children in Ukraine affected by the Chernobyl disaster.

In the new millennium, however, as we raise up mission teams and support national missionaries, my ministry has changed to focus more on strategic planning. Increasingly, Christians in Eastern Europe, whom we had encouraged, trained or supported, are beginning to carry the torch.

The reality of how our ministry was evolving struck me in the winter of 2003 when I joined a team of EEO-supported Russian evangelists on a preaching trip to remote prisons beyond the Urals, on the western edge of Siberia.

The Ural Mountains are a range in western Russia forming the geographical boundary between Europe and Asia and extending about 1,500 miles from the Arctic Ocean southward to Kazakhstan. It was there, in that barren and forsaken place, that Josef Stalin sent prisoners and dissidents into political exile. Most of the prisons still operate today, though they house criminals rather than political dissidents.

Our trip began by meeting with prison officials in Moscow before a late-night flight to Yekaterinburg in the Urals, the summer home of the Romanov Czar Dynasty. I met with the four Russian missionaries and a translator at the Yekaterinburg airport, and together we proceeded on a 9-hour drive to the small village of Sossava.

The drive to Sossava was not a quiet ride in an air-conditioned tour bus. Only those who have been on the Mr. Toad's Wild Ride at Disneyland can begin to understand the experience! Before our team squeezed into two ancient Ladas, a compact car common in Russia, the Russian evangelists talked among themselves for a while about the steering problem on the older of the two cars. They finally decided that we would get started and fix it along the way.

If I had been in charge, I might have vetoed their decision, suggested a hotel for the night, a repair shop in the morning, and a continuation of our trip after it was fixed. But these men were full of zeal for the Lord, anxious to get moving, and I was filled with God's peace as we drove into the night.

After we left the outskirts of Yekaterinburg, I was struck by the darkness of the night. In Southern California, it's difficult to escape the night glow at all. But in the Urals, the piercing darkness and brilliant stars are a stark and visible reminder of the majesty of God. I felt He was watching and protecting us as we bounced along roads that became increasingly rough the further we got from civilization.

We finally arrived in Sossava and were invited to stay in a Christian family's small apartment. They were thrilled to serve the Lord by sharing their home with us.

The apartment was actually a communal building, a single-story log cabin where several families share one roof. It was built on the frozen tundra for which Siberia is known, but that means the foundation is only strong during the winter freeze. When spring comes, the ground becomes a bog, and buildings settle. The apartment building had done a lot of shifting over the years, and stairs and hallways were at odd angles.

I made the mistake of asking to use the bathroom, not realizing that pipes were frozen and there was no running water inside the flat. The outhouse was partially submerged in the thawing mud bog. There were twelve of us in that apartment, so we entered into the life of the people we sought to serve, and endured faulty plumbing for a few days, something they put up with all the time.

The fellowship we shared was sweet during our brief stay with the family. We sat around the table and ate traditional Russian meals prepared with loving hands. Solyanka soup, cucumbers, tomatoes, pork fat, and hunks of white bread were plentiful. We found a simple stool and listened while Sergey Terentyev, one of the prison evangelists, played his guitar and sang, and each of us in turn spoke of our common faith in the Lord.

Sunday morning found us sharing God's Word and fellowship with the few believers who live in this village. Some of them were the children of prisoners exiled under Stalin. Their stories were horrific, full of hardship and tragedy. After service we drove to the local prison in Sossava, where we preached the gospel and encouraged believers who were imprisoned. As in the Book of Acts, we returned to the church that night to report on what God was doing and to share in a meal and have communion together.

At 5 a.m. the next day I was summoned by one of the missionaries. "Jeff, get up. It is time to leave. Let's go before the roads thaw from the overnight freeze!"

I rubbed my eyes and got ready for the 120-mile drive over mud-filled roads to a remote prison. The guys were gung ho, ready to seize the day. I hoped for a cup of instant coffee but there wasn't time. The local prison administration office in Sossava had evidently promised a truck or helicopter to transport us out to the prison. The day before, however, two of our men went to the office and discovered that we would be on our own. In fact, we found out later the director questioned the wisdom of trying to navigate the road at all in our two dilapidated Lada cars.

The journey was supposed to be only 2-3 hours each direction. The long Russian winter was now thawing out, making the roads impassable. Snow plows didn't seem to exist and the perilous travel conditions turned it into a two-day trip that saw us getting bogged down in mud and being rescued several times.

When noon arrived that first day, we realized we had only traveled 60 miles in seven hours. The road had started to thaw and our little Ladas floundered in the deep mud. While we were scratching our heads, trying to figure out what to do next, a four-wheel-drive jeep appeared and the driver agreed to take us all the way to the prison. To the minds of many this may not seem like a big thing, but I believe it was a genuine miracle from the Lord. We had traveled 60 miles and had not seen another car on the thawing tundra road, but at the time we needed help the most, the jeep appeared. Not only that, the man driving the jeep was willing to reverse direction so we could go to the prison and share the gospel with the spiritually hungry men there.

The four Russian evangelists were not surprised that God had acted providentially on our behalf. While they were thankful to the Lord for His timely provision, of course, I could see that these men had a very different perspective about how God works in the lives of His children. In America, even Christians would put their trust in the Auto Club, but these men of faith put their faith fully in the Lord. For me, at the time, it was a kind of illumination; these men were living Spirit-directed lives like the believers in the Book of Acts, and I was thankful that EEO could support and encourage them.

Upon our 3 p.m. arrival, the prison director expressed his amazement that we had actually made it. He was genuinely happy to see new faces in such a remote place.

Tired and hungry, and seemingly at the end of the world, it was time to summon our strength for the ministry. Miraculously, however, it was not our strength that took over. The Holy Spirit had gone before us and was already working in the hearts of these forgotten men. Fifty-five out of the 500 men in the prison filed into the cafeteria to hear the music and to listen to the message.

The men were quiet and attentive as I shared. At the invitation to come forward, 40 men responded by gathering around us in small groups to pray and ask questions. They begged for more Christian literature and asked for our missionaries to keep coming back. The spiritual hunger was amazing. Even though we did not keep to our own timetable that day, the Lord was certainly keeping us on His.

As we journeyed back to Sossava, we learned that the Lord was not finished with us. We were forced to stay overnight in a tiny village where our vehicles were stuck, and the four Russian evangelists turned it into an opportunity to share the gospel.

There was a small log town hall in the village and soon the people from the village filled it. They remarked to each other that it had been a long time since they had come together during that dreary winter, and they were happy to see each other.

After people had a chance to chat, each of us took a turn at sharing God's love for the people. We shared our testimonies and salvation Scripture, and it was a lively evening. One old communist man lectured the crowd that religion was foolishness, and a woman shared her fear that she was demon-possessed. But, at evening's end, several had prayed to receive the Lord and that brought joy to our hearts.

The man with the jeep offered us hospitality that night. We had nowhere to go, of course, and were thankful for a place to stay. We entered their log home though a lower level which was their barn. As they opened the door, the smell of the cow and other animals permeated our senses. We climbed a few more steps that led to a door, and there was a cozy kitchen behind it. The Christian woman had prepared a wonderful meal for us and we gladly ate it. That night their little home was filled with tired men as we each found a place on the floor and we fell asleep quickly in the warm surroundings.

The next morning we were up long before the sun. We had many miles to travel while the road was still frozen. But again, the road was a mess. The jeep driver pulled us for a while before giving up and turning back. Bogged down in the mud, we sat there and watched the morning light dawn on the horizon. A few minutes later a tractor appeared on the isolated road. We learned that the tractor once belonged to a Soviet collective farm, but this man had purchased it when the Soviet Union fell, and he made his living by plowing fields for others.

He was in a good mood, his vodka bottle a trusted companion in the cold tundra morning, and he dragged us out of the mire. The men did not miss this opportunity to witness; they gave him a few rubles for his trouble and shared the gospel with him. I could see him waving at us in the rear-view mirror as we continued our journey.

Our battle against the mud was not over, however. The undercarriage of the two Lada cars became so caked with mud and they just stopped rolling. The men knew just what to do. We all got on one side of a car and rolled it over to expose the underbelly of the car, and they used tree limbs to dig out the mud from around the wheels and motor. This happened several times before we reached the section of the road that was built atop the tundra and was free from the thawing sticky soil.

This was one of the most rigorous trips I had ever been on in my thirty years of ministry in Eastern Europe. But the Lord used it to teach me several things. One was the confirmation that we were using money donated to EEO in a way that pleases the Lord. It seems like there is never enough money to go around, so it is a constant challenge to invest in the places that honor the Lord the most. The money invested in the lives of the Russian evangelists and the spiritually hungry prisoners is one that will pay huge spiritual dividends. As we traveled those last few miles to Sossava, I thought about all the EEO donors who make our ministry possible. I thought they might have a joyous surprise in heaven when they saw the fruit of their giving.

The second thing that the Lord impressed upon me was that faithful men, like the four Russian evangelists, were ready to endure any hardship to share the gospel with others. I realized afresh the importance of supporting faithful men like these. The four evangelists proved to me that there are many Spirit-filled people who are ready, willing and able to take the initiative. When we supply funds to them, we are priming a pump that produces a fountain of blessings. A changing of the guard had taken place.

I am thankful for all the men and women in Russia, Ukraine, Kosovo and elsewhere in Eastern Europe who have a passion for sharing the love of Jesus Christ. EEO, together with these Christian leaders in Eastern Europe, are fulfilling God's purpose by being a conduit for His love.

Dateline Beslan, Russia, September 1, 2004. My good friend and EEO board member Pastor David Grisanti called me on my cell phone. "Jeff, have you seen the news about the school kids taken hostage in Russia? Is EEO going to do anything to help?"

The news of the hostage-taking of children was shocking. Muslim militants had taken about 1,200 people in a siege on the opening day of classes at School Number One in Beslan, and it ended with the deaths of over 330 hostages, half of them children.

Soon after the standoff between between the hostage-takers and Russian security forces ended in disaster, Pastor Sergei Danielenko, one of our ministry partners in Moscow, sent me an urgent email. He asked if we could help with a plane ticket for him to go to Beslan, and if we could supply resources for victim families and for survivors of the massacre. I immediately arranged for the things he needed.

EEO is not a relief organization. We are involved in more long-range projects like distributing Bibles and other Christian literature, caring for at-risk children and ministering to prisoners. Nevertheless, we must respond as the Lord leads to use our experience and contacts to alleviate human suffering and share Christ's love if at all possible. Kosovo was one case and the tragedy at Beslan was another one.

We ended up sending two representatives to minister in Beslan, Pastor Danielenko and Alexander (Sasha) Cherednichenko from Neftekumsk, which is located just a few hours from Beslan. They were able to meet victims, pray with them, and find out what kind of tangible help we could provide in the time of crisis.

The entire murderous hostage-taking was horrible, but I thought one of the most poignant aspects was the deaths of the children of Taymuraz and Sergey Totiev, brothers who were pastors of the Evangelical Baptist Church in Beslan.

Taymuraz Totiev and his wife lost four of their children in the massacre, including Larissa, 14, Luba, 12, Albina, 11, and Boris, who was eight years old. A daughter named Magina was found hurt but alive, and after a stay in the hospital, she recovered.

Sergey Totiev and his wife lost children too: Dzerassa, 15, and nine year-old Anna. A son named Azamat, 12 years old, was treated for a severe eye injury, but survived.

All of the children were believed to have died on September 3, the day of the gun battle between Russian forces storming the school complex and militants demanding independence for neighboring Chechnya.

The Christian testimony of the Totiev family was strong in the town. Neighbors of the family reportedly told the parents with tears in their eyes, "You lost your children, but we feel like they were our children too. They were shining lights on our street."

At the funeral for the children, people in the crowd began cursing and vowed to take revenge against the terrorists. Pastor Sergei, who lost two children in the siege, stood up at the end of the service and reportedly said, "Yes, we have an irreplaceable loss, but we cannot take revenge. As Christians, the Bible teaches us that we must forgive. Vengeance is in God's hands." The crowd was very moved by Pastor Totiev's words.

The whole situation was perplexing to me. It seemed incomprehensible that terrorists would be so brazen as to target children. At the same time, I had a burden to help, and EEO sponsors had made that possible though their financial gifts. The question was, what could we do to help people deal with the nightmare that had overwhelmed them? EEO pastors Sergei and Sasha had done what they could by praying and counseling with families, and helping them with food and other immediate needs, but it seemed we could do more. I felt I should visit Beslan myself to see what else we could do, so with a staff member, I headed for Russia. This journey left an indelible imprint on my heart and mind.

We arrived in Vladikavkaz on a flight from Moscow. The first day we had meetings with our contacts there, then drove out to Beslan to visit the school. I entered the courtyard by the gymnasium where so many had died and saw bottles of water everywhere. They were all covered with a light mantle of snow from the first winter storm. The water bottles were memorials left by towns-people for those who were held hostage and were denied water for three days by the cruel terrorists.

I was actually surprised at the size of the gymnasium when I entered it. It was so small, yet it had held over 1,200 hostages. I looked at the many hand-written memorials on the walls, the blown-out windows, and then my eyes fixed upon the twisted basketball hoop. The terrorists had placed a bomb on the hoop, and when they triggered it on the third day, many died instantly in the explosion. The explosion caused armed volunteers from Beslan, along with Russian troops, to attack the building, and many of the hostages died in the ensuing gun battle.

I moved from the gymnasium through a door that led to the classrooms, which were filled with schoolbooks and rubble. The terrorists had taken children to these rooms and molested and tortured them. As I walked along the hallway to the cafeteria, I saw hundreds of bullet holes from guns fired both by terrorists and those who tried to liberate the hostages.

The cafeteria was a somber place. It too was filled with rubble, the place where the terrorists had herded children to gun them down as their negotiations with President Putin's government began to falter. The terrorists wanted freedom for Chechnya, but it was out of the question to the Russian government. The children became the pawns of Muslim demands, demands that could never be met.

The next day we drove to the Beslan cemetery. To the left was a large old cemetery which had served the needs of Beslan's families for generations. Next to it was a new cemetery, filled with fresh graves from the atrocity. There were only sad images there. As I walked along the rows I viewed the photo of the person buried there; a photo had been attached to nearly every cross by family members. The graves of the children were particularly sad, not only because of the photos of young faces, but because of the teddy bears and other stuffed animals that family members had left for their darling children. At some graves, parents sat sobbing. It was a heart-breaking experience.

Before I left the cemetery, I stopped at the place where all the Totiev children were buried. I paused and prayed for their families, and I also prayed that God would intervene and change the lives of the black-hearted people who were so willing to commit such unspeakable crimes against children for political gain.

As I lifted my head and opened my eyes, I knew it was time for me to leave the cemetery behind, and to see what we could do for the living. After what I had seen, I could only imagine the spiritual, emotional and physical pain the survivors were experiencing, but I felt God wanted EEO to have a part in healing the wounds.

Along with a helper from a local church, my team and I started visiting survivors in their homes. We listened to their stories, and we asked what we could do that would help most to relieve their suffering. The stories were all heartrending, but during our visits we were able to show the love of Christ. Each family, without exception, was glad that we had gone to their home to show our love and concern.

One thing did surprise me, however. When we asked what we could do to help, many said they wanted to get away from Beslan and all its horrid memories for a while. They didn't care where they went; they just wanted to escape. Since many of the families were dealing with their grief and not working, I thought food or money might be high on their list of needs, but it turned out that release from their agony was most important to them. They needed to be in another place so they could gain some perspective on what had happened in their lives.

Many Russians have a desire to visit Western countries, and we were able to arrange a trip to Finland headed by EEO missionary Zaven Pogosov. They went to a Christian camp where they received grief counseling in a private setting. They also had the opportunity to visit museums and shops. The children went to a water park, and some of them laughed for the first time since the tragedy at their school.

As part of this program, we helped these people gain some biblical perspective on their suffering. It was wonderful when some of them asked the Lord into their hearts and lives. There was a baptism service for these new believers before they left Finland to return to their homes in Beslan.

My experience in Beslan was further evidence to me that a changing of the guard was taking place. Even though our world is now enmeshed in the politics of terrorism, we need to remain steadfast in our work of sharing God's love even though we must do it in hard places during difficult times.

I have to admit that sometimes I feel a little distant from our war on terror in America. Terrorism is horrifying and devastating for those who experience it, but for many people it is little more than a flickering image on television. However, when I walked through the halls of School Number One, and smelled the flowers on the graves of the children of Beslan, I felt the impact of evil in our world in a new way. I resolved again in my heart to do everything I could to see people come to Christ while there is still an opportunity.

15
FULL CIRCLE

On each step of this journey of faith I have simply tried to do God's will as I understood it, to be obedient to His vision as I saw it. But as you reflect upon the past you see things in a new way. As we go through life, our human limitations only enable us to view our experiences as a tangle of threads, like the back of a tapestry. It is not until we walk around and view the tapestry from the front that we are able to see the beautiful picture. When we look at the picture from the front, we see our lives as God intended them. Things have a way of coming full circle.

Recently I had the joy of visiting with Colonel Alexander Nikolaiyevich Dolgich in Moscow, and we were able to sit down and talk about many of the events that had transpired during the days when he was Director of Youth Prisons for the Russian Federation, and we were supplying food and spiritual sustenance to incarcerated young people. There were many things that transpired back then that had puzzled me, and Colonel Dolgich, now an independent investigator for the Ministry of Justice, was freer to talk about the past.

His new role as an independent investigator and the prospering economy in Moscow allow him and his wife Lydia to now live in an upscale apartment in central Moscow. When I contacted him about coming for a visit he invited me there for dinner and casual conversation about the experiences we had shared.

We both laughed a bit as we talked about our first meeting, a time when we were both sizing one another up.

One of the things that had always interested me was his personal views on the fall of the Soviet Union and the rise of the Russian Federation. After all, he had spent his career as a Soviet officer, and I was interested in his perceptions of *Glasnost* and *Perestroika*.

His views were illuminating. He said, "I thought personally that it was just a change of party, but that the structure of our government would not change. After all, I was military and we did not take part in a political revolution, so things did not change for me in my work. On a personal level I had normal hope for the future, but Gorbachev did not inspire any special hope for the future in me."

The paternalism of the Soviet Union forced a kind of trust in the government, and this turned out to be a good thing as Gorbachev instigated change; as long as people at the top of the power pyramid were happy with what was happening, it would trickle down to all levels of government, including the military. Everyone in the Soviet Union was accustomed to following orders.

Our conversation drifted to spiritual matters, and I asked him a question that was on the minds of many Americans during the Cold War. Was atheism just part of the "party line," or did individuals continue to privately embrace Christian faith and values?

Colonel Dolgich replied that he thought that area of life was mostly influenced by family. He said, "My parents were products of atheist propaganda and our generation was the result."

There were two events that caused me to think that perhaps Colonel Dolgich had departed from atheism: one was the time he raised his hand to be saved when I preached to a group of prisoners, and the other was the time he sang a Christian hymn with such vigor on our ride to the airport. These, of course, are not the normal actions of someone who has renounced God. So, at our meeting, I asked him very gently about what was going on in his mind when he raised his hand during the preaching service, trying to discern whether he had actually asked the Lord into his life.

Colonel Dolgich said, "While you were preaching you told the group, 'God loves you all and looks at you like people, not prisoners. He sees what is in your heart.' I agreed with everything you said. It was sincere and it touched my heart as well as the hearts of all the people in the auditorium. I knew I needed the forgiveness you were talking about."

During our conversation, Colonel Dolgich revealed something that touched my heart, and apparently had been on his mind for a long time. He reminded me of our visit to the Mozhaisk prison and the picnic lunch on the Borodino battleground. He said, "You know, there is a Russian Orthodox monastery on the grounds very near the prison. In all my years as director, the priests never showed any interest in visiting the young prisoners. It took someone from the other side of the world like you to come help them."

We returned to Germany in 2003. It was like a trip in a time machine. Our two eldest children had been born there, and our daughter Lindsey accompanied us. We had not been back to Berlin since January 1990, just 60 days after the Wall had come down.

In Berlin we visited a few families that we used to smuggle Bibles to. We hadn't seen them for thirteen years.

One night we decided to surprise one Bible smuggling contact, the Strauss family. Detlev and Heidi still lived in the same house on a quiet street in south Berlin. About 7 p.m. we found their home. As always, the gate was locked. I rang the bell and out walked an older gentleman with gray hair. "Is that Detlev?" I whispered to Paula and Lindsey.

The gentleman walked out to the gate and blinked a few times in the dark. He opened the gate, stared for a moment, and exclaimed, "Bob and Mary! Is that you?" Back in Bible smuggling days, we had used fictitious names to protect our contacts and ourselves in case of interrogation by the authorities. Paula and I were always known as Bob and Mary to our East German friends.

We hugged, laughed, and entered their home. We shared our real names with them, which caused a little confusion. All night long, they didn't quite know what to call us. Finally Mr. Strauss said, "Look, we understand your real names are Jeff and Paula, but to us, you will always be Bob and Mary! We do not know you any other way." They had been the contact for their small church and we had all loved the times we could spend together back then.

"Detlef, were you ever followed or interrogated by police during the years you received Bibles and literature? Did they ever ask you about us?"

"No, no, of course not. Look, it wasn't against the law to have friends from the West. And besides, we always distributed the literature very quickly."

"I will say, though, that one team your mission sent to us insisted on unloading their camper right in our garage. We were nervous at the time since they came during daylight hours. We didn't want our neighbors to see that foreigners had come to visit us but the Lord was faithful to protect us and your mission."

"What did you guys do when the Berlin Wall came down?" I asked. "We looked for you dancing on the Wall on CNN!"

"Our 16-year-old son, Christoph, came home from school and told us a rumor about the people being allowed to visit West Berlin. We immediately turned on the television to a West German channel. We couldn't believe our eyes as people streamed through the border. Christoph and his friends headed for Friedrich Strasse to see if it was really true. *Die Wende* ("the change") is definitely a highlight in our lives."

We returned the next evening to meet their children and have dinner together. Detlev is still involved in mission work and now makes an annual mission trip with his church to Ukraine. They too, like EEO, are helping orphans and prisoners while working with local churches there. Paula and I had such fond memories of the Strauss family, and had always wondered if they felt the same.

Our surprise visit on this cold January night rekindled our friendship and assured us their feelings were the same. They were and are a family we could have been much closer friends with had we lived under different circumstances.

After a few tears, hugs, and an exchange of email addresses we sadly said our goodbyes. This solid Christian family continues to march as soldiers in God's army. Both in good times and bad, in freedom and in persecution, they have remained faithful to the Lord.

On our return visit we also saw another family, Pastor Kurt Rogalski and his wife Brigitte, who had been particularly active under the communist regime. He was a man of faith, and his gray hair had not dimmed the sparkle in his eye. Kurt pastored a small Baptist church in East Berlin during our years there and we had become good friends. I woke them on many late-night visits stealthily carrying Bibles and books up the stairs to their small apartment. They always prayed for our safety and a special bond of serving the Lord knit our hearts together.

LEAVING THE AMERICAN SECTOR

Pastor Rogalski always had a heart and vision for young people. He led worship playing piano quietly in his living room, did Bible studies with them, and his home was a secret hub of activity where young people could "hang out." My visits to him were always after 10 p.m. so the neighbors wouldn't know he was receiving a visitor from the West. His ministry with young people was illegal at the time, and his neighbors kept an eye on him as good Party members were supposed to do.

Living in freedom these past years has been both a blessing and a curse. His church pension is small. They don't own a home. He doesn't think like a West German—in modern business ways—he thinks like an East German, like someone who was a prisoner most of his life.

Brigitte spoke with Paula as she dished up bowls of soup for us in the kitchen. Graying hair and wrinkled skin could not extinguish the sparkle in her eyes. They now lived a simple life, and she accompanies Kurt as he conducts church services in mainly former East German cities. Despite their financial hardship their love for the Lord had not subsided.

After a lunch of soup, sandwiches, and fresh bread, we spoke about the the Eastern German Secret Police, called the Stasi, and the files they kept on their citizens. I asked directions to the office where I could file the application to see my file. Kurt knew exactly where to go as he shared that he too had requested his file and received it several years previously. He retrieved the file, sat down, and set a large three-ring binder on the coffee table.

"Bob," he said, "they had over 300 pages about me in their files. They confiscated my mail. They listened to my telephone calls. They reported on the sermons I preached. My neighbors gave reports about my activities."

As Paula and I sat next to them on the couch, we felt sad and privileged to even be in the same room with this couple.

Paging slowly through their secret police file was like watching a slow-motion version of the old television show "This Is Your Life." We felt sad because their best years had been served under threats of prison and persecution. We felt privileged because we were in the presence of true heroes of the faith.

He pointed to a letter in the file. "Look here," he said, "my father wrote me a letter." It was still in the original envelope. He opened the letter and read it.

Dear Kurt,

I know we are living in difficult times. I am thinking of you and I know times are tough for you. Keep looking to Jesus. Keep your eyes fixed on Him. Remember that in your circumstances He is with you and He will never leave you. I want to give you these verses to think about and be encouraged by. I love you, son.

Your Dad
APG 1:8 und 1Kor 13

Kurt removed his glasses and wiped his eyes with a handkerchief. "The secret police believed my father was sending me a secret message, a code," he said. "As an enemy of the State, they could not allow this letter to be delivered to me, and they had to find out what the secret code was. An agent was assigned to the task of breaking the code and reporting back to his superiors."

Kurt continued. "Here is the report by the agent. Look how very detailed he describes his methods to break the secret code. The agent went to the central library of East Berlin and asked for assistance from the chief librarian. Together they found a Bible on the shelf in the Religion section. This agent figured out that the APG at the bottom of the letter was actually an acronym for Apostelgeschichte (the Book of Acts). He looked up chapter 1 verse 8 and wrote it down right here:"

But you shall receive power when the Holy Spirit comes upon you; and you will be my witnesses in

*Jerusalem, and in all Judea and Samaria, and to the
ends of the earth.*

"I have broken the secret code," the agent wrote. The
agent had also looked up 1Kor 13 (1 Corinthians 13)."

Kurt looked at us with grief in his heart and eyes and
continued. "My father included the Bible passages in his letter to encourage me. When I got this precious letter from my
father, it was 17 years after he had written it. I found it in
this file. He had already been dead for three years. I never
got to thank him for his letter, for his encouragement, for his
kind words and uplifting spirit. The communists kept us in
prison and stole that which was most precious to us. And
yet, in God's plan, He had a secret police agent reading the
Bible and writing down Scriptures, breaking God's secret
code. It is so amazing how God works in our lives."

Pastor Kurt, now in his 70s, had every reason to be bitter, hardened by life's circumstances. Instead, he and
Brigitte are still serving Jesus with joy in their hearts.
Before we left that day, we all gathered in the small living
room and sang a German hymn to Jesus while Pastor Kurt
skillfully played the piano. I flashed back to a late-night
visit many years before behind the Iron Curtain. Worship in
the life of Pastor Kurt is something that never changed. I
pray that my own life will impact others just as Pastor Kurt
Rogalski's example has impacted mine.

As I reflect on the past, I am reminded that the ministry
of EEO has grown and been enhanced through the efforts of
Godly men that the Lord has brought to us over the years. I
am thankful that each one was with EEO for a season before
being prompted by God to start their own ministries. Just as
with Paul and Barnabas, the separation was not always
smooth, but, as a result, the end the Kingdom of God has
been expanded.

Jim Manning, now of Mission Assist, was the first missionary co-worker to join EEO staff. His arrival coincided with moving the office out of our home to quarters over a pizza place in Canyon Lake, California. Jim led teams to Bulgaria for us and continues to serve the Lord around the world from his home office in Arizona.

Soon thereafter we were joined by David LeCompte, whom I met at our home church of Calvary Chapel Murrieta. David joined EEO to help recruit and lead teams to teach in the Russian youth prison ministry. He left EEO to start a ministry in Chechnya and is the founder of In His Fields, Inc., in Pennsylvania.

Bill and Mary Agius joined EEO after making a mission trip with us to Romania. They served in Germany and Holland for several years before returning to start Christian Comfort International. They now lead a new ministry near Colorado Springs.

Wes Bentley, the president of Far Reaching Ministries, also got his start with EEO after a preaching trip to Russian prisons. Wes was part of our staff for three years before making a trip to Sudan with Pastor Gary Kusonoki of Calvary Chapel Rancho Santa Margarita. Pastor Gary made his first mission trip with EEO before starting the church and today is the mission president of Safe Harbor, Inc. Wes continues to work in Kenya, Uganda and Sudan, and Far Reaching and EEO enjoy a great relationship.

During those exciting early years after the fall of communism, George Bryson, who is now Director of Calvary Chapel Church Planting Mission, helped me recruit mission travel teams through our radio programs on KWVE and KKLA in Southern California. George has been leading church planting teams to Russia now for many years but we continue to encourage one another in this wonderful world of overseas missions.

I am thankful for the contribution each man has made to the EEO ministry and for their friendship over the years.

16
INTO THE FUTURE

What does the future hold for Eastern European Outreach? It would be wonderful to be able to look into the future and know God's will. However, the situation is much more complicated. We walk by faith, not by sight, and my prayer for the future is that we continue to walk by faith and hear the voice of God as He directs us.

What will Eastern Europe be like in the year 2025, and how will EEO be ministering to people? There is only one sure thing and that is, if the Lord tarries, we will still be seeking to win people to Jesus Christ and to disciple them into a Christ-centered life.

Beyond that, the situation gets complex. If you would have asked me 20 years ago how we would be ministering to people in Eastern Europe today, I would have described for you a huge Bible smuggling operation strategically supplying a network of committed churches. There was no way that I or anyone else could have predicted the fall of communism. I consider the demise of communism to be one of the great miracles of our modern times. That and the emergence of the Church in China after the Cultural Revolution shows the amazing power of our sovereign God in the lives of human beings.

That is perhaps why Proverbs 16:9 is important, "In his heart a man plans his course, but the LORD determines his steps." While I desire God to determine our steps on a day-to-day basis, events are now taking shape in Eastern Europe that will very likely affect what we will be doing in the future.

Today's generation of children represents the future for all countries, and especially for Russia and Ukraine. Our God-given mandate at EEO is to do all we can to reach this generation of young people with the gospel of Jesus Christ. After we have reached them, we are to disciple and nurture them to spiritual, physical and emotional health, helping them become future leaders and impact their countries for Christ.

Why are we focusing on today's younger generation? Many people do not understand that Russia is in a state of social disintegration. The average life expectancy of the Russian male is only 58 years old, less than people born in impoverished Bangladesh. In 1991, when the Soviet Union collasped, the Russian population was 149 million. It is expected that by 2050 the population will continue its downward spiral by one million people per year to 100 million people. Even this is an optimistic government projection, and others believe that the population will only be 75 to 80 million.

Of Russia's current population there are close to one million orphans. The prison population is just as large or larger. Today in Russia heart disease, alcoholism and tuberculosis are epidemic. An even greater threat on the horizon is the specter of SPID, which is the Russian acronym for AIDS. The World Bank estimates that by 2020 at least five million people in Russia will be HIV-positive. Independent research foundations believe that to be very conservative, and that the figure will be closer to 14 million people. Imagine a Russian population in 2020 of 130 million people, of which 14 million are HIV-positive.

Russia and Ukraine are both mired in a negative population growth pattern combined with a sharp increase in HIV and communicable diseases. Today's young people must encounter the transforming power of the gospel if their generation is to turn around and truly impact the future of these once proud countries. EEO has been very successful, with the generous help of our child sponsors, to keep children out of orphanages and at home with a mother or guardian. Now, however, God is calling us to raise our vision to the next level and tackle the obstacles keeping these same children and others like them from reaching their full potential in Christ.

Most experts, including those at the Center for Disease Control (CDC) in Atlanta, believe it will be at least a decade before the full force of the AIDS epidemic is felt in Russia and Ukraine. If these dire predictions come true—as all appearances indicate they will be—the majority of future orphans EEO will be caring for will be HIV-positive orphans. The time for vision and action is now.

Ukraine won its independence from the Soviet Union in 1993 but the situation there is strikingly similar to that of Russia. A beacon of hope, however, and the greatest thing that has occurred in recent Ukrainian history, is the December 2004 Orange Revolution and the election of Viktor Yuschenko. Yuschenko became famous for his disfigured face and the story of his poisoning with dioxin, which made headlines around the world.

Former president Leonid Kuchma, who was a Russian

puppet, was in power for eleven years and sought to maintain his power by personally selecting his successor, Viktor Yanukovich. Yanukovich, a Russian, came from Donetsk and was backed by the communist-leaning hard-liners who blamed Western nations for the social ills of their once-proud country. Widespread fraud and stuffing of ballot boxes took place by Yanukovich's followers in the December election.

Within days of the falsified results being announced, the people of Ukraine rose up and began to peacefully fill the streets of downtown Kiev, the capital of Ukraine. Government offices were closed off as access was blocked by protestors. A tent city emerged as 500,000 people filled the downtown area wearing orange scarves and caps signifying their loyalty.

The Orange Revolution, however, has lost its steam amid political infighting and corruption. President Yuschenko strongly supports religious freedom and closer ties with the West. However, the political party of his arch-rival, Viktor Yanukovich, now commands a large percentage of the popular vote. So the struggle continues and there is no way that we can know the outcome. The only thing that we can know for sure is that there is a great deal of instability in Ukrainian society and the potential for chaos remains.

To me, however, this means that we have an even greater opportunity to reach people for Christ. In the midst of great political instability and social disintegration, God has called EEO to share His message of hope and forgiveness.

As we move forward, confident in the knowledge of His will, we want to understand the present as we prepare in faith for the future.

In the future, we want to expand our minstry in four key areas: Child Sponsorship Ministry, Foster Family Orphan Assist Program and the Education Opportunities Initiative.

We also want to maintain our Christian camp program as a top priority, and to enhance it.

The EEO Child Sponsorship ministry is designed to help keep at-risk children at home with at least one parent. It is the only ministry approach I know of that really intervenes and provides critical support to a mother or guardian so as to keep their child out of an institution.

We monitor every family with our network of loving coordinators, and thus keep tabs on how families are doing. I believe the first step in preventing more children from becoming social orphans is to identify and assist these at-risk families. Sponsorship will continue to be a vital component of our ministry.

Child abandonment is at epidemic proportions with conservative estimates at over one million orphans in Russia and Ukraine. Ninety percent of these children are "social orphans" meaning that they have at least one parent still living, but they have been removed from the home for their protection. The future looks bleak for the social orphans of Russia and Ukraine. The statistics suggest that the number of children under state authority will keep growing radically.

Foster care is almost unknown in Eastern Europe, even though it has had real success in America. When children have been abandoned in Eastern Europe they are warehoused in orphanages. In America, our social welfare agencies place children with foster families who then receive financial support from the local county or state in which they live.

According to the U.S. Department of Health and Human Services, 59% of children placed into foster care are adopted by those who take them in. If these types of statistics could be repeated in Eastern Europe, it would mean that the population of orphanages and youth prisons would be reduced by half. Of course there is an economic barrier in Eastern Europe because families there do not have the financial resources to support foster children, nor do they receive support from the government for this purpose.

Our goal would be to mobilize and train Christian foster parents in Ukraine and Russia to address the problem of almost one million social orphans. When dedicated believers there learn about the plight of local orphans they are often willing to help. Thousands of Christian families in Russia or Ukraine would be willing to take in a child in need if they could afford it. But with cramped living conditions and poor finances, most people do not see how they can help.

I believe EEO and Foster Family Sponsors can make a difference by matching American sponsors with a foster family overseas. Again, the spiritual and physical connection through prayer and support are the tools the Lord uses to bring healing and hope back into the lives of these abandoned orphans. EEO will network with other organizations and churches to develop an effective long-term approach which will have government approval. Loving Christian foster families are the answer to the social orphan epidemic in Russia and Ukraine.

The Education Opportunities Initiative is one that we began to implement during the 2004/2005 school year. As children have grown up and graduated from our child sponsorship program, they have been faced with a lack of opportunities to pursue higher education. Developing strong

Christian leaders means providing young people with opportunities they never dreamed were possible.

EEO has many wonderful qualified students eligible for scholarships who do not have sponsors. This is a relatively new ministry for EEO and one which we are committed to see expand in the coming years. In Ukraine, though the cost has risen, the average cost for one year of higher education varies from $1,000-$2,500 per year, over 10 times cheaper than in the United States. What a great investment in the future of Ukrainian Christian leaders!

One aspect of the educational process is mobilizing young men to mentor and disciple orphans and those in youth prisons. This vision has been growing in my heart for quite some time. As a result of my own ministry of teaching and preaching in Russian youth prisons, I have recognized the great need for Christians to be raised up to mentor younger ones.

We want to connect sponsors in the U.S. with mentors in Ukraine and Russia to encourage them in prayer as they befriend young people at risk.

The cycle of despair for children at risk must be broken at all costs. Salvation and growth in Christ is our first priority and emphasis. Secondarily, however, we are compelled to do what we can to provide education opportunities that will allow them to impact their future families, churches and communities for Christ.

The bucolic village of Doragynka, ninety minutes south of Kiev, Ukraine, provides the backdrop for the soon-to-be built EEO camp and retreat center. Nestled on ten gently rolling acres bordered by forest and small farms, this recreational center will provide a refuge of safety and hope for children at risk.

Besides children's camps, the center will host conferences

for men, women's retreats, and discipleship weeks. Sports, vocational training, and biblical training seminars are all part of our future plans. Even small-group foster homes are planned for this idyllic location.

In the coming years, we want to put a renewed emphasis on ministry to women. Eastern Europe is filled with strong women. One of the reasons they must be so strong is because their husbands have abdicated their responsibility to build strong families. All too often husbands are alcoholic, violent and apathetic. They don't feel they have a future because of the economic situation in the former Soviet Union, so they replace nurture and productivity with drunkenness and machismo.

It is this mindset that EEO would like to address. We think we can make a difference by building strong families with a two-pronged effort—first by providing a training ground for boys and girls, strengthening them, and second by offering retreats, seminars and adventure camps aimed at men of all ages. This new Doragynka camp facility will exist to help all family members in a distinctive way.

Once families have a spiritual foundation, all things become possible, whether it be the challenges of the prosperity or the social upheavals that may yet come. It is a matter of caring for at-risk children here and now—both those who are able to remain in their family of origin and those who may become part of a new foster family. It is also goes one step beyond and seeks to imbue men with a different mindset, a mindset that honors Jesus Christ. This empowers them to have strong families themselves and to be a positive influence on them and on society at large.

Prisoners, widows and the poor are with us always. It is the desire of our heart at EEO to continue to show the love and compassion to these people as Jesus has asked us to do. More than just maintaining the status quo in the future, we hope to go one step further by seeking to build people up. To let children know that they are not alone, to be an encouragement to them as they live the Christian life and to fulfill their personal aspirations. We want to help mothers or grandmothers raise their children, so the children do not have to go to live in the street or in an orphanage. We want to let men know that being a reliable husband and father is something that pleases God and is the pathway to personal happiness.

Jesus calls us to introduce people to Him and to disciple them. That has not changed in the past 2,000 years and will not change until the day the Lord returns.

At EEO, we want to be found taking care of the Father's business until He returns.

Faith in Christ is the substance of things hoped for, the evidence of things unseen.

You are invited to visit

www.LeavingTheAmericanSector.com

This is a special Web site where you can discover more about Jeff and Paula, and Eastern European Outreach.

The Web site contains additional information, including the story of "Operation Andreas," launched against Jeff by the East German Secret Police (Stasi) in the 1980s. This information has only recently come to light.

The site is also filled with missionary stories and pictures, and has information about how you can become a short-term missionary yourself.

There are also some great articles about children's lives that have been changed through the power of Christian love, and about how you can participate in the EEO Child Sponsorship program.

It's an exciting and inspirational Web site, so visit today!